RACERS 1969–2000

The Legends of Formula 1

Gilles Villeneuve, Ferrari, 1977–1982

ALAN HENRY

RACERS 1969–2000

The Legends of Formula 1

QUEENSGATE PUBLICATIONS

First published in 1999 by Queensgate Publications, Cookham, Berkshire

ISBN 1-902655-02-8

A catalogue record of this book is available from the British Library.

Acknowledgements – and grateful thanks – are due to John Townsend of F1 Pictures, John Dunbar and Karen Sutton of Zooom Photographic, and Paul Vestey of the GP Library. The photographs in this volume were drawn from these three collections.

Design by Production Line, Minster Lovell, Oxford
Production by Landmark Consultants, Princes Risborough, Buckinghamshire
Printed in Singapore

Front cover photograph **A study in concentration: Ayrton Senna**

Contents

Foreword

THE ERA OF GRAND PRIX RACING represented by the drivers in this volume spans one of the most exciting periods in the sport's history, with its growth in popularity rising to the point where it is now the most popular global televised spectacle.

There are many Racers within Alan Henry's book whom I identify as close friends, several of whom drove for me with notable success during my 18-year ownership of the Brabham Formula 1 team. There are also too many names no longer with us, which serves as a stark reminder of just how dangerous motor racing was in the late 1960s and early 1970s – and just how much progress we have all made in improving safety over the past couple of decades.

I am a firm believer that Grand Prix racing should be the pinnacle of our sport, yet that is no reason for it to be unacceptably hazardous. I have always campaigned for improved track and car safety, and I am proud of the manner in which the FIA, motor racing's governing body, has progressed this and continued to investigate new ideas to improve the current standards. If I have a regret, it is that too many drivers featured in this book never lived to benefit from the secure environment which Grand Prix racing now takes for granted.

Bernie Ecclestone

Bernie Ecclestone
Knightsbridge, London

Opposite page Monaco, 1999: Michael Schumacher scores his fourth victory in the Principality, which remains the spiritual home of the instinctive Racer.

Racer to his very core: Keke Rosberg – the original 'Flying Finn' – displayed an acrobatic driving style that thrilled enthusiasts the world over.

Introduction

YOU DON'T HAVE TO BE NUMBERED among the greatest of Grand Prix drivers to be regarded as a Racer. Any sportsman has his own quota of God-given aptitude and skill; how he harnesses and deploys such attributes can make all the difference. Formula 1 motor racing is a sport – a business, if you like – which is full of subtleties. On the face of it, one driver is pretty much like another. But the reality is substantially more complex than that.

This volume offers a selection of driver portraits from across the most significant Grand Prix generation in the sport's history. Thirty years during which the sport changed more than in any other period.

It begins at a time when death and risk were inextricably bound up as an accepted element of this always-hazardous pastime. Despite the admirable efforts of men such as Jackie Stewart, who rammed home the point that top-line drivers were being paid to demonstrate skill rather than run disproportionate physical risk, when Grand Prix racing moved into the 1970s it was still a business where death was expected and, more to the point, *accepted* by the outside world. In the summer of 1970, for example, three leading international drivers were killed within the space of three months. The accidents that claimed Piers Courage, Bruce McLaren and Jochen Rindt – the World Champion-elect – hit the headlines for just a couple of days. But when Ayrton Senna was killed at Imola, 24 years later, the sense of moral outrage – fed by the popular press – lingered in the air for weeks. Attitudes in the outside world had certainly changed, even if the Racers had not.

The subjects in this book are laid out in broadly chronological order, relating to the years through which they raced with most success – not results, necessarily, but more the moment when promise was fulfilled. Starting with Jochen Rindt and ending with Mika Hakkinen, they are all Racers to a man. Drivers who pushed that little bit harder. Men prepared to take surprising risks. Motivated sportsmen who emerged from the cockpits of their cars radiating the inner confidence of a job well done.

Of course, they were not miracle workers on each and every occasion they accelerated away from the pits. In that respect some readers might be baffled by the candidates I have reviewed, such as Carlos Reutemann. Surely his overall career performance was too patchy? This is not the point. Granted, the quiet Argentine driver could have days when he looked as though he was taking his time. Just as John Watson sometimes looked as though he had lost the plot, so Niki Lauda could appear plain lazy and Nigel Mansell furiously over-drove his machinery on more than one occasion. But none of this prevents them from being bracketed as Racers.

Every man in this book has delivered more than was expected from him, more than once, at various stages of their career. They are men who have tackled the high wire. Some may have wobbled ominously, but they all gave it their best shot.

ALAN HENRY
Tillingham, Essex

Jochen Rindt

THE FREEZE-FRAME IMAGE will remain fixed for all time in the minds of those enthusiasts whose passion for motor racing was shaped in the late 1960s. The scene was a rain-drenched Silverstone. The occasion, the 1969 International Trophy race, that popular curtain-raiser to the European Grand Prix season in the days before commercial pressures rendered the non-championship Formula 1 race extinct.

A misfiring engine had dropped Jochen Rindt's works Lotus 49B almost to the tail of the field in the opening stages of the race but, as the engine began to run cleanly again, the Austrian ace piled on the pressure. Deftly powering the red, white and gold Lotus across the glistening puddles in a series of nonchalant, opposite-lock power slides, Rindt tore through the pack to finish a close second to Jack Brabham's out-of-fuel Brabham-Repco at the chequered flag.

This was just the sort of race performance that encapsulated the story of Rindt's career: hero of the hour, but seldom a winner. Only in the last 11 months of his life did he finally latch onto the run of success that he, together with his contemporaries and rivals, always knew he had in him. Finally, with the 1970 World Championship within his grasp, he was killed at Monza, when his Lotus 72 crashed during practice for the Italian Grand Prix.

Rindt enjoyed more than a passing degree of financial independence. Born on 18 April, 1941, his

parents were killed in a bombing raid on Hamburg when he was just over a year old. He was subsequently bought up by his maternal grandparents in the provincial Austrian city of Graz, eventually inheriting the Mainz-based spice mill, Klein and Rindt, which had been founded almost exactly 100 years before his birth.

Consistent success only came with a move to Team Lotus in 1969, although Rindt's relationship with Colin Chapman was fragile.

Campaigning the Cooper-Maserati at Monaco in 1966.

Opposite page **Jochen Rindt in 1965 – his first full season of Formula 1.**

One season with
Brabham, in 1968,
yielded just two finishes.

The young Rindt was a wayward, independent lad. He grew up among a group of similarly well-heeled, yet reckless, youngsters in Graz. One member of this crowd was Helmut Marko, who would later go on to compete in Formula 1 for BRM. 'In those days,' Marko reflected shortly after Rindt's death, 'we belonged to the same gang, but we weren't very considerate towards one another.'

Rindt's great hero was the German Ferrari driver Wolfgang von Trips who, with bitter irony, was killed at Monza nine years before Jochen suffered the same fate. The following year, 1962, Rindt began racing Alfa Romeo saloons, and moved up to the cut and thrust of Formula Junior in 1963.

In 1964 he visited the London Racing Car Show. Cutting quite a dash in a long camel hair coat, the 22-year-old Austrian produced a cheque for £4,000 with which to purchase a Formula 2 Brabham. Within months he would catapult into the racing headlines, using this car to win the Whit Monday Formula 2 International at Crystal Palace.

'New star shines at the Palace' boomed the newspapers. 'Young Australian *(sic)* beats the established stars!' Clearly the headline writer could hardly believe a non-Commonwealth driver could display such genius. Either way, Jochen's star was in the ascendant.

Sure enough, his Formula 1 debut was not long in coming. He was invited to take the wheel of a private Brabham-BRM in the 1964 Austrian Grand Prix, held on the runways and perimeter roads of the Zeltweg military airfield in Styria. The car was owned by the legendary private entrant, Rob Walker. He remembers being charmed by his new young driver:

'Our plane landed at Graz,' recalls Rob, 'and Jochen was waiting to meet us. It was so sweet. He was like an excited schoolboy. He drove well in the race, and

Opposite page
With the faithful Lotus
49B at Clermont Ferrand
in 1969.

wanted to drive for me in 1965. But I advised him to accept an offer of a works Cooper drive. In those days private entrants like us had to qualify, but works teams had a guaranteed entry.'

So, at the end of the season, Rindt signed a three-year contract with the British Cooper team. Unfortunately, Cooper's fortunes were in gentle decline by this time and Jochen failed to realise his potential during 1964–65, the final two years of the 1.5-litre engine regulations.

He did, however, share the winning Ferrari 250LM with Masten Gregory in the Le Mans 24-hour sports car race. They started 11th, and had moved up to eighth by the end of the first hour. Jochen handed the car over to Masten after about 90 minutes, but two hours later the bespectacled American driver returned to the pit lane with a misfiring engine.

'That's it,' thought Jochen, and began packing his bags. But the Ferrari's distributor was changed, and the car readied again for battle in just over half an hour. Gregory found Jochen in the paddock car park, trying to extricate his hemmed-in rental car. 'We can't lose, if you think about it,' said Gregory. Jochen agreed that they should resume, but only on condition that they went flat-out, win or bust.

For the rest of that epic race they thrashed the Ferrari to within inches of its life. During the chase through the field it consumed six sets of tyres and brake pads. But they won. 'That mad sonofabitch Jochen,' was how Gregory would always affectionately remember his Austrian colleague.

In 1966 the new 3-litre Formula 1 engines arrived, and Rindt's Cooper enjoyed something of an Indian Summer using an uprated version of the Maserati V12 engine which had originally been used in the famous front-engined 250F almost a decade earlier. His most spectacular performance came during the

Rindt's first
Championship points
for Lotus came in the
1969 British Grand Prix
at Silverstone, where
he finished fourth.

With Ronnie Peterson
in 1970. It was the
Swede's first season
in Formula, and would
be Rindt's last.

Open-faced helmets offered minimal protection, while seat harnesses had only just become fashionable… Formula 1 was overdue for change.

ill-starred Belgian Grand Prix at Spa-Francorchamps. Most of the field had been eliminated in a series of accidents – caused by an unexpected opening lap deluge – and Rindt himself survived an 150mph pirouette on the Masta straight before battling with John Surtees's Ferrari and eventually finishing in second place.

He finished third in the 1966 World Championship, the best placing of his career so far, but no Grand Prix wins came his way and he eventually decided to leave Cooper, for Brabham, at the end of 1967.

Jack Brabham's team had won the previous two World Championships, and Jochen was attracted to the idea of a straightforward, uncomplicated and reliably-designed car. On paper, the partnership should have been a success. The new Brabham BT26 followed in the superb-handling wheeltracks of its predecessors, but the latest four-cam Repco V8 engine was hideously unreliable. Jochen managed a third place in the South African Grand Prix – in the 1967 car – after which a

fourth place at Nürburgring and pole position at Rouen-les-Essarts, for the French Grand Prix, were the only highlights of a disappointing year.

Yet Rindt admired Jack Brabham enormously. He put his trust in the laconic Australian and respected his dedicated professionalism. More to the point, because Jack was in the other car, Jochen found driving for him reassuring. It was a relaxed, pleasant partnership.

Jochen may not have won Grands Prix yet, but he kept his reputation alive in the hard-fought world of Formula 2. Driving for Winkelmann Racing, he became king of this prestigious second division. But it wasn't enough.

Towards the end of 1968 he began receiving overtures from the Lotus boss, Colin Chapman. The legendary Jim Clark had been killed in the spring and, despite Graham Hill raising the team's morale by taking the World Championship, Lotus was badly in need of an inspired top driver to replace the Scot.

Engine specialist John Judd, who was working on Brabham's Repco programme, recalls Rindt as 'a bloody good sport.'

'We had no aggro with him at all,' he said. 'Of course, he got browned off with everything, but he knew we were working bloody hard on the engine.' Brabham's business partner, Ron Tauranac, echoed those sentiments: 'Jochen was always very 'pro-us' at Brabham,' he remembered. 'When he was offered a deal to go to Lotus he came to us, told us what Chapman was offering, and said that he would stay (with Brabham) for a fraction of the price. He was a good bloke.'

Eventually, however, Chapman's bid would so commandingly eclipse anything that Brabham could offer that Rindt felt he had no option but to sign. He was hungry for success. He even said to Rob Walker: 'You know, Rob, I want to win the World Championship so much, I'm even prepared to drive a Lotus.'

He had been married to Nina – the daughter of Finnish millionaire and amateur racer Curt Lincoln – for eighteen months, and in August their only child – a daughter – was born, christened Natascha Jonin. The Rindts were a glamorous couple, setting up home in Switzerland where their close neighbours included fellow racers Jackie Stewart and Jo Bonnier. Stewart and Rindt would soon become close, their friendship underscored by a mutual respect and the knowledge that they were the best Formula 1 drivers of their era. Even so, Stewart would admit that he found Jochen

and Nina 'very European' in a way that was almost disconcerting. 'Helen and I were surprised when they would argue in public,' he recalled with a grin. 'It was something which a couple of conservative young Scots like us would have never dreamed of doing!'

Rindt went into the 1969 season armed with the Lotus 49B, now in its third season of racing and getting rather long in the tooth. Stewart's new Matra-Ford MS80, entered by Ken Tyrrell's team, was a much more competitive machine and Jochen's frustrations continued. He was also lucky to escape with only a hairline skull fracture after the rear wing of his Lotus collapsed while he was leading the Spanish Grand Prix.

His initial apprehension over the constructional delicacy of Chapman's cars seemed to have been justified. For his part, the Lotus boss didn't really understand him. Accustomed to an almost telepathic, fraternal relationship with Jim Clark, Chapman now found himself dealing with an abrasive and impatient personality in the Austrian. The situation was not helped when immediate success failed to come Rindt's way.

At the British Grand Prix, the pair argued bitterly over which cars the team should use. Colin wanted his men to drive the radical four-wheel-drive Type 63, but Rindt was having nothing of it. He insisted on using the regular 49B, and forced Chapman to borrow back one of the cars from Swiss privateer Jo Bonnier (to whom it had been sold). Jochen duly qualified on

A sensational victory at Monaco in 1970, where Rindt pressured his former team-mate, Jack Brabham, into a mistake on the last lap, set the Austrian on the path to the World Championship.

pole position and became embroiled in a sensational battle for the lead with Jackie Stewart's Matra. The two men were in a class of their own as they streaked away from the field. This time, Jochen was on course for victory only for the rear wing end plate to work loose, prompting a brief pit stop. He resumed in second place, then had to stop again for more fuel, and eventually finished fourth. 'Driving for Lotus is like being with Barnum and Bailey's circus,' he shrugged.

Veteran British journalist Denis Jenkinson summed up the feelings of many when he said: 'Rindt has not yet won a Grand Prix, and I'll bet my beard he never will.' For Jenks, who had partnered Stirling Moss on their legendary winning drive in the 1955 Mille Miglia, this was indeed tempting fate. At the end of 1969, Jochen finally broke his duck with victory in the United States Grand Prix at Watkins Glen. Jenks' razors were duly sharpened!

For 1970 Chapman produced the sensational Lotus 72, with torsion bar springing, a sleek chisel nose, side radiators and inboard brakes. Rindt's air of apprehension about the car was palpable. The 72 took a long time to develop and Jochen, in the interim, used the old 49C – now in its fourth season of racing – to pull off a memorable victory in the Monaco Grand Prix.

Cruising around in the midfield during the early stages of the race, Jochen suddenly came alive towards the end when he caught a sniff of possible victory. Clocking record lap after record lap, he went into the final lap only a couple of seconds behind his old pal, Jack Brabham, in the BT33. All the way round the gruelling Monaco track Rindt seemed to haul back

yards on every corner, but it still seemed as though Brabham would make it.

Then, unbelievably, the veteran Aussie became flustered. He locked up his brakes at the final corner and skidded straight on into the straw bales. Rindt had pressured him into a crucial error and nipped through to win.

By mid-season the Lotus 72 was ready to race competitively. Jochen took it to a commanding victory in the Dutch Grand Prix, at Zandvoort, but it was a victory marred by the death of his friend Piers Courage, whose de Tomaso crashed and burst into flames. Rindt began thinking seriously of retirement if he won the World Championship.

Further victories followed in France, Britain and Germany. He failed to finish the inaugural Austrian Grand Prix, at the new Österreichring circuit, but still led the Championship points table going into the Italian Grand Prix. There at Monza – late in Saturday afternoon qualifying – he took the Lotus 72 onto the track shorn of both front and rear wings in an effort to match the straight-line speed of the more powerful Ferrari 312Bs.

Approaching the Parabolica at around 175mph, the Lotus began to fishtail under braking. It speared off to the left and struck one of the vertical wooden uprights supporting the guard rail. Rindt, who did not use crutch straps, suffered the most grievous neck and chest injuries.

The man who had the World Championship in his pocket died in the sordid confines of an Italian ambulance later that afternoon. He became the sport's only posthumous Formula 1 Champion.

Rindt's air of apprehension about the revolutionary – and untested – Lotus 72 was almost palpable, although there was no denying its competitiveness.

Jackie Stewart

JACKIE STEWART CELEBRATED HIS 60TH BIRTHDAY in June 1999. And yet the retired triple World Champion's demeanour could hardly be further removed from that of a potential pensioner. He still has the jaunty walk, the irrepressible conviviality and the boundless energy which he channelled to brilliant effect on his way to three world titles with Tyrrell in 1969, 1971 and 1973. Now, a quarter of a century after he hung up his helmet, Stewart is a multi-millionaire – and on first name terms with royalty no less. But, with his delightful self-deprecatory humour and high standards of business behaviour, he has retained the common touch.

In recent years, Stewart and his family have provided a contemporary legacy to the sport by producing a new crop of talent. Paul Stewart Racing, named after his eldest son, helped shape the racing careers of stars such as David Coulthard and Dario Franchitti. The success of the team led, perhaps inevitably, to the establishment of their own Formula 1 operation, Stewart Grand Prix. But Jackie himself has left an even more enduring memorial to motor sport.

It is easy to forget that, in the 1960s, racing drivers were killed almost every weekend of the year. These personal tragedies were usually marked only by brief obituaries in the motor sport magazines and with little in the way of further comment. The possibility of being killed was a real risk for a professional driver; Stewart determined to change all that. Almost single-handedly, he debunked the myth that racing drivers should be devil-may-care extroverts, who shrugged aside the risk of a fatal accident with the careless insouciance of a Spitfire pilot. His was a brave stand, prompted in part by an accident during the 1966 Belgian Grand Prix on the epic Spa-Francorchamps road circuit.

An unexpected storm, only a couple of miles into the race, saw the bulk of the grid eliminated. Cars skated off the track in all directions, but by far the most serious incident involved the BRM driven by Stewart, then one of the sport's most promising young rising stars.

'We just ran into a wall of water,' he remembers. 'I must have been doing around 165mph when the car aquaplaned and I lost control. First I hit a telegraph pole, then a woodcutter's cottage. I finished up in the outside basement of a farm building. The car ended up shaped like a banana, and I was still trapped inside it.

'The fuel tank had ruptured inwardly and the monocoque literally filled up with fuel. It was sloshing around in the cockpit. The instrument panel was smashed, ripped off and found 200 metres from the car. But the electric fuel pump was still working away. The steering wheel wouldn't come off and I couldn't get out.'

Stewart was eventually helped from the wrecked car by his BRM team-mate, Graham Hill, and Bob Bondurant. He sustained four broken ribs, a broken shoulder bone and pelvic injuries in what was the worst accident of his professional career. It also prompted the Scot to recalibrate his approach to the sport. Racing drivers, he reasoned, should be paid to demonstrate their skill, not simply their bravery, in what – in retrospect – seem prehistoric conditions.

On his return to racing, Stewart became the first Formula 1 driver to use a seat harness. He also ensured thereafter that a spanner was taped to the steering wheel of his BRM, in order to facilitate his escape in the event of a similar accident. He embarked upon a crusade for improved circuit safety, which earned him the respect and grateful appreciation from successive generations of Grand Prix drivers. By the time he retired in 1973, the old Spa-Francorchamps circuit had been sacrificed. It no longer made sense to race at 175mph down country lanes with such limited protection. The world was moving on.

Born in Dumbarton on 11 June 1939, Jackie was written off academically at an early age. Many years later he was diagnosed as suffering from dyslexia but, despite the scholastic problems stemming from this disability, he quickly proved himself to be an adept sportsman. Between 1959–62 he won the British, Scottish, Irish, Welsh and English trap shooting championships and only just missed making the Olympic team.

'I think the difficulties at school gave me a determination to succeed, because among my peers I was considered stupid at a time when school was such a central, essential part of life,' he reflected. 'I left

school at the age of 15, and served petrol in the family garage for a year. I earned more in tips than I did from my wages, but I ran the best forecourt in the county. Then I went into the lubrication bay, and made sure you could eat your breakfast off the floor. That was a good experience, because for the first time people praised me.

'When I started shooting, at the age of 14, I was suddenly provided with something at which I could excel. Those years were enormously important for the formation of my thinking processes, in dealing with competition and with success and failure.'

Jackie began racing on an amateur basis, but during a test at Goodwood he caught the eye of the Track Manager, Robin McKay. That in turn brought him to the attention of the man whom would do so much to shape his career, Ken Tyrrell.

Ken invited him to drive for his Formula 3 team in 1964. The Tyrrell-entered Cooper-BMC ran away with the British Formula 3 Championship, and the next thing Jackie knew he was being courted by some of the top Grand Prix teams in the business. Colin Chapman offered him the chance to team up alongside Jim Clark at Lotus. But Stewart declined the offer, correctly judging that Lotus was Jimmy's personal fiefdom, and that making his own mark there would be extremely difficult. Instead he signed with BRM to drive alongside Graham Hill. By any standards it was a perspicacious move, enabling Jackie to consolidate his reputation as the most promising Formula 1 newcomer for years.

His maiden Formula 1 outing came in the non-championship Rand Grand Prix, on Johannesburg's Kyalami circuit, at the end of 1964. He started from pole position for the first of the two heats, but broke a driveshaft on the line. That meant he had to start at the back for the second heat. Incredibly, he tore through the pack to win. The wee Scot's genius behind the wheel had certainly moved seamlessly across the divide between Formula 3 and Formula 1.

He was back in South Africa, East London this time, the following month for his maiden BRM outing. He finished sixth, scoring a World Championship point on his Grand Prix debut, before returning to Europe to qualify on pole for a non-title race at Goodwood. He also won the International Trophy at Silverstone – beating off a challenge from the Ferrari of the reigning World Champion, John Surtees. He finished the year in style with his first Grand Prix victory, at Monza.

In 1966 he picked up where he had left off the previous year, with a win at Monaco in a two-litre Tasman BRM V8. But the onset of the three-litre regulations saw the team bogged down with technical problems. BRM pinned its hopes on a hopelessly complex and unreliable H-16 cylinder engine and, although Jackie kept his name in the spotlight with a brilliant drive to second place at Spa in 1967, it was not enough to sustain his profile.

By the end of 1967 he had an offer on the table from Ferrari, but chose instead to throw in his lot with his old pal Ken Tyrrell. The Surrey timber merchant had forged a partnership with the French

Jackie of all trades: his versatility included sports car racing for Ecurie Ecosse with this Cooper-Monaco.

Regular success came first with Ken Tyrrell's Matra, pictured here at Brands Hatch in 1968.

The Cosworth-powered Matra took Stewart to within a whisker of the 1968 World Championship, which was lost to Graham Hill.

chassis manufacturer, Matra, and was now set to start his own Formula 1 team. He asked Jackie how much he would need as a retainer. The answer came back: '£20,000.' Tyrrell reached for his cheque book.

The 1968 season got off to a troubled start. His Tyrrell Matra MS10 ran out of fuel in the closing stages of the Belgian Grand Prix – a race he had dominated. In fact, it was a feature of Jackie's career that some of his best drives failed to yield victory. A minor accident in a Formula 2 Matra saw him fracture the tiny scaphoid bone in his wrist. It took 20 weeks to heal, during which he raced with a temporary plastic cast fitted to his wrist. After wrestling the Tyrrell Matra to sixth place in the 1968 British Grand Prix, at Brands Hatch, Stewart had to be lifted from the cockpit. He flew home to Geneva and slept without stirring for 18 hours.

'I was totally used up, and it would have been very easy during that race for me to stop,' he explained. 'Just to finish sixth and earn one point didn't make much different to the outcome of the Championship. But it might have done. Had I given up, I would have learned how to give up, and that's a lesson I never want to learn. It's so easy, such a comfortable route to

JACKIE STEWART

Heading for victory, and another World Championship, in the Tyrrell-Ford at Paul Ricard in 1971.

On the limit at Monaco in 1972, where he won three times.

nowhere. The devil on your shoulder says, 'Oh, wouldn't it be lovely to pack it in? Let's go home early and get into a bath.' But once you've done it – human nature being what it is – you will do it again.'

Stewart was often subjected to critical barbs from those who believed he was a member of the 'milk and water' brigade, whose obsession with safety was somehow devaluing the sport. But two of the three races Stewart won in 1968 were in conditions of torrential rain, at Zandvoort and the Nürburgring, where he proved he was no soft touch when it came to the business of high speed precision driving. He lost that year's Championship at the final round in Mexico, the title going to Graham Hill and Lotus, but in 1969 he made no mistakes.

He won the South African, Spanish, French, British, Dutch and Italian Grands Prix to take the Championship in storming style. It was a performance that emphasised just what a natural talent he possessed. The car control flowed from his finger tips and – like all the truly great racing drivers – while he was able to analyse and itemise the mechanics of car control in specific detail, the real speed and flair came from a natural, instinctive sense of balance and co-ordination.

Jackie increasingly proved to be an outstandingly cerebral sportsman. He could use his brain to work out a performance advantage ahead of the game. One such example of this came at Monza in 1969. Contemplating the gearing of his Tyrrell Matra, he realised that time was lost changing up from fourth to fifth on the sprint from the final corner – Parabolica – to the finishing line. He calculated that if he fitted a high fourth gear then he could hold that all the way to the line, and not lose those vital fractions involved in

Right Stewart became one of the most well-known sportsmen in the world.

that extra gear change. Involved in a classic slipstreaming battle with Jochen Rindt's Lotus, for the lead of the race, Stewart kept this card up his sleeve until the last lap. Rindt pulled level on the run to the chequered flag, but Jackie used his technical advantage and just hung on ahead of the Lotus to win the race and clinch his first title.

In 1970, Matra wanted to go it alone with its own V12 engine. The French company would have been delighted had Tyrrell and Stewart agreed to use it, but both wanted to stay with the Cosworth Ford DFV.

The Spanish circuit at Montjuich Park, in Barcelona, in 1973. Stewart would claim his third world title at the end of this season, before announcing his retirement from Formula 1.

With Jack Oliver *(left)*
and Graham Hill in 1969.

That left Tyrrell looking for a chassis. The financial munificence of the Ford Motor Company enabled Ken to purchase a trio of March 701 chassis, one of which Stewart drove to victory in the Spanish Grand Prix at Jarama. But long before then, Stewart and Tyrrell had concluded that the car was a dud. In great secrecy, Ken commissioned the design and manufacture of his own Formula 1 car.

The first Tyrrell-Ford 001 was ready to race in the late summer of 1970, and was fully tested and developed in time for the start of 1971. Now Jackie really hit his stride. He won the Spanish, Monaco, French, British, German and Canadian Grands Prix to take his second title. His Monaco triumph – in particular – serving to underline his enormous versatility.

The defence of his World Championship was blighted by the need to miss a handful of races in order to recuperate from the effects of a gastric ulcer. Yet again, the hard-boiled brigade who had chastised him for his safety movement went into top gear. Now, they accused, he was making himself ill because he was spending too much time trying to make money on the back of his racing. As if it wasn't bad enough that he didn't want to be killed, he also wanted to make money from the sport as well!

Stewart was fully recovered in time for the 1973 season and, using the short-chassis Tyrrell 006/007 cars, secured his third World Championship in a season when the Lotus 72s should have hung onto the title which Emerson Fittipaldi had won for them the previous year. Stewart was better than ever by this stage, fully seasoned but without losing his competitive edge. Yet for much of the year he nursed a secret, kept even from his wife, Helen. He was going to retire at the end of the season. Only Ken Tyrrell and Ford's Walter Hayes were permitted to share this knowledge in the strictest confidence.

It was during that final year that we were treated to a demonstration of Stewart's unique qualities on a personal level. His Tyrrell team-mate, François Cevert, was developing in leaps and bounds and, by the middle of the year, Jackie realised that he was now quicker than him. After the German Grand Prix at the Nürburgring, where Jackie and François finished 1–2 in what was to prove Stewart's last win, the Scot climbed from the cockpit and immediately said: 'François could have passed me any time he liked.'

Stewart had a great affection for his protégé while, for his part, Cevert simply worshipped Jackie. The Tyrrell succession seemed secure until, less than 24 hours before Jackie was due to drive his final race, François was killed in a horrifying accident during qualifying for the US Grand Prix at Watkins Glen.

The Tyrrell team withdrew from the race and Jackie Stewart retired with 99 Grand Prix starts to his credit. The rest of his life was about to begin.

Jo Siffert

JO SIFFERT'S GREATEST DAY came at Brands Hatch, in July 1968. For it was there, beneath an overcast summer sky, that he scaled the pinnacle of personal achievement by winning the British Grand Prix at the wheel of Rob Walker's Lotus 49B. He beat Chris Amon's Ferrari in a straight fight, to secure what stands in the history books to this day as the last Grand Prix victory to be achieved by a genuine private team using an 'off-the-peg' racing car.

Siffert was not the greatest driver of his generation, although on his day he was a formidable competitor, but he was one of the most versatile and determined of performers – demonstrating race-winning form not only in Formula 1, but also in the gruelling discipline of endurance racing. On top of that he was a supremely popular man, with an endearing 'little boy lost' quality to his character.

Born on 7 July 1936, Jo Siffert was the son of a car dealer from the Swiss provincial city of Fribourg. In his teens he was obsessed with the desire to own a motor cycle, and funded this dream by picking and selling flowers – as well as collecting spent Swiss army shells and cartridges to sell for recycling. He began serious motor cycle racing in 1957, before switching to cars in 1960. By 1961, he had become a consistently successful performer on the European Formula Junior circuit, using his own Lotus 20. Eventually, with the support of the Swiss Ecurie Filipinetti outfit, he acquired a Formula 1 Lotus 24 fitted with a four-cylinder Climax engine. This was to prove the start of something big.

In the 1960s the international calendar was peppered with a succession of non-championship Formula 1 races right across Europe. They did not always receive full entries from works teams, but they did offer the privateer a good chance of shaping up against the established stars. Siffert took full advantage of these races to spring a series of surprises on the Grand Prix élite long before that day of glory at Brands Hatch.

Siffert had initially attracted the attention of the Formula 1 fraternity at Pau in 1963. He did well in his private Lotus-BRM to run third, before spinning off with brake failure. A week later he finished second to Jim Clark's Lotus, and then won the Syracuse Grand Prix in Sicily. A year later – now using his own Brabham-BRM – he beat Jim Clark's works Lotus around the fast Enna-Pergusa circuit, in central Sicily, to win the 1964 Mediterranean Grand Prix. And the year after that, his car now entered by Rob Walker, he repeated the feat – his winning average speed of 139.21mph being the quickest for any Formula 1 race run up to that point.

'The one that got away' was the non-title 1965 Syracuse Grand Prix. Siffert was leading not only Clark, but also John Surtees's works Ferrari. He was actually pulling away from the pair when his car jumped out of gear over a bump and its engine mortally over-revved. Clark won the race after Surtees retired; the Scot later confided to Rob Walker that the battle between Siffert and Surtees had been so intense that he had been more than happy to sit back and watch from a safe distance.

Siffert's resilience was displayed at the next race, Goodwood's Easter Monday international. He crashed heavily at the chicane and, despite an initial assessment that he had escaped unscathed, a subsequent

'Dear Seppi' negotiating the fearsome Karrusel, at the Nürburgring, in Rob Walker's Lotus 49B.

Opposite page
Campaigning his own Brabham BT11 at Spa-Francorchamps in 1964.

He finished third at
Monaco in 1969 – his
best result around the
principality.

Siffert's prowess as a
sports car driver – seen
here celebrating victory
with Vic Elford at the
Nürburgring 1000kms –
meant that he was in
great demand from
teams such as Porsche
and Ferrari.

examination revealed that he had not only broken his ankle, but his back as well. Just five weeks after this accident he finished sixth in the International Trophy at Silverstone. Heroism, or what?

Throughout the 1965 season, Rob Walker had entered two cars for Siffert and Bonnier – but the cost of being involved in Formula 1 as a private entrant was dramatically increasing. With the onset of the new 3-litre regulations, at the start of 1966, Rob finally decided he would have to scale down his operation to a single car. He purchased a new Cooper-Maserati T81 and asked Siffert to drive it. Bonnier was understandably put out, particularly as his initial reaction was: 'What's going to happen to Siffert?'

'I'm going to have him drive my car,' replied Rob. Impassive as ever, Bonnier remained quiet for a few moments and never mentioned the issue again.

Rob Walker and his wife, Betty, grew enormously fond of Siffert during his time racing with them; the team was very much a family affair. Rob had enjoyed some wonderful times with Stirling Moss in the late 1950s and early 1960s, and now here was the chance for him and his family to rekindle something of that magic with Siffert. In Rob Walker's own biography, one chapter is titled: 'Dear Seppi'. Jo had been nicknamed 'Seppi' for as long as anyone could remember, and his tribute summed up the regard in which this quintessentially British employer held the Swiss driver.

After that clutch of non-championship victories in 1965, the 1966 season proved to be more frustrating. Even the works Cooper-Maseratis hardly represented

the cutting edge of Formula 1 technology, and the privateer's cars were probably another step down. That year Siffert managed just one top six finish, fourth place in the United States Grand Prix.

Walker stuck with the Cooper-Maserati for 1967, during which Siffert notched up two more fourth places, in France and the USA, but for 1968 Rob reasoned that he urgently needed a more competitive car. He persuaded Colin Chapman to sell him a Lotus 49 and thus began a sequence of jumbled events that would lead to Siffert's Brands Hatch triumph.

The season began on a catastrophic note. During practice for the non-title Race of Champions, also at Brands Hatch, Siffert slid off the road and wrecked the new car. The debris was immediately returned to Rob's race headquarters at Dorking, Surrey, only for a second disaster to unfold. While the chassis was being dismantled, a stray spark triggered a massive fire that destroyed Rob's entire workshop. Not only were the Lotus's remains destroyed, but Rob's entire racing archive and his priceless ex-Dick Seaman Delage were consumed by the inferno. It seemed quite possible that this might be the end of the road for Rob Walker Racing. But Betty Walker's brother, Sir Val Duncan, then Chairman of Rio Tinto Zinc, immediately wrote out a cheque for £15,000 to keep Rob in the Grand Prix business.

Although a brand new Lotus 49B was ordered, it would not be ready for some months. In the meantime, Walker and Siffert made do with an ex-factory 49 which Colin Chapman had supplied, while at the same time guaranteeing that the new car would be ready in time for the British Grand Prix.

Siffert's second – and final – Grand Prix victory came in the BRM P160 at the Österreichring in 1971, the year of his fatal accident.

It was. Just. As practice got underway at Brands Hatch, so the Walker mechanics were putting the finishing touches to their sleek new machine. Siffert rose to the occasion splendidly, qualifying fourth behind the works Lotus pair of Graham Hill and Jackie Oliver and Chris Amon's Ferrari. He ran third from the start, but when the two factory 49Bs wilted the Swiss surged into the lead. Amon stepped up the pressure and made a great race of it, but 'Seppi' refused to buckle under the pressure of the moment. After just over two hours' racing, the dark blue Walker team Lotus, with its distinctive white nose band, swept through Clearways to win by just over four seconds.

Siffert would stay with Rob Walker through to the end of the 1969 season, taking second place in the Dutch Grand Prix and a brilliant third at Monaco, a success achieved by dint of such magical, effervescent opposite-lock motoring as can hardly be imagined. One of the epic racing shots of the 1960s was taken at Massenet corner – the right hander leading into Casino Square – during that race. It depicts Siffert piling on right-hand lock as if he were driving a touring car. His was certainly an indomitable spirit.

Yardley-BRM P160
at Monza in 1971.

By 1969, Siffert was also a valued member of the Porsche endurance racing team and his contribution was regarded as absolutely central to the German company's competition efforts. The season had been his most impressive so far. Sharing the works Porsche 908 with Brian Redman, he won at Brands Hatch, Monza, Spa, Nürburgring and Watkins Glen, as well as the first Austrian 1000kms race to be held at the Österreichring, where he drove one of the fearsome new Porsche 917s alongside Kurt Ahrens.

In the sports car arena, Ferrari was pitched head-to-head against Porsche and the Italian team came up with a superb offer for 1970. 'Name your price,' said the emissary from Maranello, knowing that Ferrari could offer both Formula 1 and sports car drives. Porsche, in response, resolved to pay for Siffert to have a competitive Grand Prix seat if that meant retaining his services. BRM, Rob Walker and the new March team were all keen to have him. In the end he signed for March – paid for by Stuttgart – feeling that it was better to have the resources of a factory operation behind him. It was a disastrous relationship that lasted for only a year. Then, in 1971, he signed a contract with BRM.

In this new role, Siffert found himself ranged alongside Pedro Rodriguez, the fiery Mexican who was also his team-mate in the JW Gulf Porsche 917 squad. The two men were ferocious competitors – at Spa that season they banged doors repeatedly as their 917s jostled for track space through Eau Rouge – but both retained a healthy sense of mutual, professional respect. After Rodriguez was killed at the Norisring, while enjoying a German club race in a private Ferrari 512M, it was left to Siffert to boost the team's morale.

He did so in magnificent fashion, by leading the Austrian Grand Prix from start to finish. The win helped place him fourth equal with Jacky Ickx in the 1971 World Championship. Once the main season was over, Siffert took part in the non-championship Formula 1 race at Brands Hatch, held to celebrate Jackie Stewart's second Championship crown. The Swiss qualified his elegant, Yardley-livered BRM P160 on pole position, but made a poor start and dropped back into the middle of the pack. By the end of lap 15 he was up to fourth, but then never came round again. From the start/finish line, an ominous column of oily smoke could be seen rising over the trees against the dazzling blue early autumn sky.

The BRM had apparently suffered a rear suspension failure in the 160mph dip before Hawthorn Hill, effectively endowing it with rear-wheel steering in a split-second. The car slammed into the earth bank at the side of the track, flipped over on its back and then flew over a marshal's post. It landed upside down again and burst into flames. There was no chance for Siffert, who perished in the wreckage.

Only three years and three months had passed since 'Dear Seppi' had been cheered, by thousands of fans, to victory in the British Grand Prix – at that very same circuit.

Opposite top Siffert and Rob Walker were forced to borrow a factory Lotus 49 for the 1968 Belgian Grand Prix at Spa-Francorchamps, after a fire destroyed Walker's workshop.

Opposite bottom A Porsche-funded drive with the uncompetitive March 701 in 1970 proved disastrous.

Jacky Ickx

IN THE HALF-CENTURY SINCE THE INCEPTION of the World Championship, there has been a handful of drivers whose talent was so obvious that a title crown seemed to be their due, yet who encountered a crucial set-back which prevented them from realising that supreme achievement. Stirling Moss is the most obvious example. Less well remembered, perhaps, is Jacky Ickx, who got close enough almost to taste the celebratory champagne in both 1968 and 1970.

Born in Brussels on New Year's Day, 1945, Jacques-Bernard Ickx was the son of a respected Belgian motoring journalist. Young 'Jacky' initially contested motorcycle trials events before switching to four wheels, where he gained quite a reputation at the wheel of a Lotus Cortina. He moved up into Formula 3 and soon caught the eye of Ken Tyrrell, who promoted him into his Formula 2 team, in 1967, to contest the European Trophy series in a Matra MS7.

Ickx duly won that series to consolidate his reputation as a brilliant new talent. Yet it was his performance in the Formula 2 category of that year's German Grand Prix that really stopped the clocks.

Jim Clark had qualified on pole position, with a best lap of 8m 4.1s around the epic 14-mile circuit. Alongside the Scot's Lotus 49, on the front row of the grid, were Denny Hulme's Brabham (8m 13.5s), Jackie Stewart's BRM H-16 (8m 15.2s) and the Eagle-Weslake of Dan Gurney (8m 16.9s). The slowest Formula 1 qualifier was privateer Guy Ligier, whose Brabham-Repco had lapped in a leisurely 9m 14.4s.

For the sake of the Formula 1 drivers' self-esteem, it was just as well that the Formula 2 class lined up separately behind the main Grand Prix grid. Ickx was the fastest Formula 2 contender, lapping the Tyrrell-Matra in 8m 14.0s. This was not only a full 20 seconds quicker than the next fastest Formula 2 runner, Jack Oliver's Lotus 48, but it was also quick enough to have qualified him third for the Grand Prix proper!

The reality of the situation was that the nimble Formula 2 Matra was a vastly more driveable proposition round the Nürburgring than many of the 1967-vintage Grand Prix cars. Even so, it was an impressive performance.

There were 17 Formula 1 cars ahead of him at the start, but he was already up to 12th by the end of the

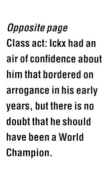

Ickx's Grand Prix debut came at Monza in 1967, where he brought a Cooper-Maserati home in sixth place.

Opposite page
Class act: Ickx had an air of confidence about him that bordered on arrogance in his early years, but there is no doubt that he should have been a World Champion.

Ickx's best years were with Ferrari, 1968 and 1970-73, although a collision with Jack Oliver at the Spanish Grand Prix in 1970 nearly killed him.

Heading for second place at Montjuich Park one year after the accident.

opening lap. Superbly exuberant driving saw him climb as high as fourth place before the Matra's suspension broke. His cocky confidence seemed to be running at such intensity that Jackie Stewart, having retired his BRM with transmission failure, actually went down to the Tyrrell pit to suggest that Ken call in his young protégé before he did himself some harm. Tyrrell listened politely, but declined to follow Stewart's advice.

Interestingly, although Ken was highly impressed with Ickx, he noted that when his Formula 2 team entered for races where a graded driver was permitted to compete – and in Tyrrell's case that

meant Jackie Stewart – the young Belgian was not quite so impressive.

'He did not star quite so much when Jackie was around,' Ken recalled. 'But even so, we wanted to take him into Formula 1 as our second driver in 1968. However, Matra made it clear that they would only make a single Ford-engined chassis available for Jackie. We couldn't find a place for Ickx.'

At the end of the 1967 season, Ickx was invited to drive a third works Cooper-Maserati in the Italian Grand Prix. He finished sixth, scoring his first World Championship point. That performance set him up nicely for a move to Ferrari for the following season. He was just 23-years-old, and already conscious of his celebrity status.

He was paired alongside the easy-going New Zealander, Chris Amon, who had joined the Maranello squad the previous season. Jacky immediately seized the upper hand in his relationship with his team-mate. Somehow, the new boy managed to avoid doing much of the work when it came to testing, and Amon did not particularly appreciate having to run-in Ickx's cars at Modena prior to the races. His ambivalence towards his colleague was not helped when Amon discovered that Ickx was picking up a bigger pay cheque. 'I went to see Mr Ferrari and said: 'Hey, what's all this about?' And he paid up,' remembers Amon. 'I suppose it was my fault for not pushing harder.'

Ickx cemented his status within the team by scoring a brilliant victory in the French Grand Prix at Rouen-les-Essarts. In torrential rain, he led virtually from start to finish. It was one of several high points in an impressive maiden Formula 1 season for the Belgian driver, who hung onto a mathematical chance of taking the Championship as the teams crossed the Atlantic for the Canadian Grand Prix. Unfortunately, those aspirations came to an end during practice for the race when a sticking throttle caused Jacky to crash heavily, breaking his leg below the knee.

At the end of the 1967 season Ickx switched to Brabham, which ran on the same Gulf oil and Goodyear tyres as the JW endurance racing team for whom the Belgian also wanted to compete. He finished the 1968 Formula 1 season in fourth place, and improved to second the following year – albeit a long way behind the new World Champion, Jackie Stewart. But Ickx did score a decisive victory over the Scot in the German Grand Prix at the Nürburgring, as well as a second – more controversial – win in Canada, where he pushed Stewart's Matra off the road.

That season also saw Jacky score a sensational victory in the Le Mans 24-hour race. Having walked – rather than run – across the road to register his disapproval of the traditional Le Mans starting procedure, Ickx had been last away in his Gulf Ford GT40. As things transpired, it mattered little. Remorselessly, he and co-driver Jack Oliver hauled themselves back into contention, and Ickx beat Hans Herrman's Porsche in a last lap shoot-out to score one of the closest-ever victories in the French epic.

In 1970, Ickx decided to return to Ferrari. His initial tests with the new 312B1 – powered by a flat-12, three-litre engine – left the Belgian with a broad smile on his face. 'It felt very strong, smooth, torquey – and extremely powerful,' he grinned. There was no question in his mind that here was a car capable of getting on terms with the best of the Cosworth-powered opposition.

Yet the new Ferrari had a shaky start to 1970, sorely testing Ickx's resilience. The Spanish Grand Prix, at Madrid's Jarama circuit, was also marked by one of the closest escapes of his career. With his car heavy with fuel, Jack Oliver's BRM suffered a front stub axle failure on the opening lap and T-boned Ickx's Ferrari on the approach to a downhill hairpin. The impact ruptured the fuel tanks and both cars were enveloped in flames. Both men emerged more-or-less intact, but Ickx suffered some unpleasant burns to his hands.

Mechanical problems would blight Ickx's efforts during the first part of that season. He qualified on pole for the French Grand Prix at Clermont Ferrand, only for engine trouble to intervene shortly before the start and consign him to an inevitable retirement after just 16 laps. He led again at Brands Hatch, only for the differential to fail, and then battled wheel-to-wheel with Jochen Rindt's Lotus 72 to take a close second place in the German Grand Prix at Hockenheim. Finally, he took the 312B1 to its maiden victory in the Austrian Grand Prix, at the Österreichring, heading home team-mate Clay Regazzoni. But he was not able to carry this success through to the Italian Grand Prix, where his car succumbed to clutch failure. At least Regazzoni's victory saved the day for the home team.

After Rindt's death, the only way in which Ickx could deprive his former rival of the Championship crown was to win all three remaining races on the calendar. He came incredibly close to pulling it off. In the second half of the 1970 season, the elegant new Ferrari 312B1 was not just the quickest car in the business, it was also one of the most reliable.

He won the Canadian Grand Prix, and was on course to win the penultimate race – at Watkins Glen – when a leaking fuel line lost him too much time. Despite a brilliant recovery, from 12th to fourth at the

Forever the 'nearly man' of Formula 1, Ickx came close to Championship glory in 1968 and 1970. By the middle of 1971, however, his Ferrari was growing uncompetitive.

finish, Rindt's posthumous crown was secure. But it was a close shave: Ickx won the last race of the season at Mexico City, and closed to within five points of the late World Champion's total.

Incredibly, Ickx would win only another two Grands Prix during the remainder of his Formula 1 career. He triumphed in Holland in 1971 – another example of his extraordinary wet weather car control – and then won the following year's German Grand Prix at the Nürburgring. It was only five years since that head-turning performance in the Formula 2 Tyrrell-Matra.

There was one more glorious Grand Prix moment left before the Belgian's single-seater career went into gentle decline. At the wheel of a Lotus 72, he splashed to a memorable win in the 1974 Race of Champions, at Brands Hatch, taking the lead from Niki Lauda's Ferrari with a stunning lunge round the outside of Paddock.

From 1976–78, Ickx drove intermittently for the small Ensign team before being given one final chance with Ligier, in 1979, after Patrick Depailler broke his legs in a hang gliding accident. The best he could manage was one fifth and a sixth place. At the end of the year he finally called it a day, although there was still plenty of endurance racing success to come. He won Le Mans for the last – sixth – time in 1982, at the wheel of a Porsche 956.

Jacky Ickx was one of the most enigmatic drivers of the post-war era. On a personal level he had great charm, laced with the unruffled distant formality which

one tends to associate with the over-privileged. Some say he was rather spoiled, only rising to the occasion when an event was going his way. But when he did give it 100% – particularly with the rain sheeting down – a quite remarkable talent went on display.

Mario Andretti

THE YOUNG BOY LEANED ON THE HANDLES of his bicycle and craned his neck to get the best view as the silver roadster – carrying the red-painted race numbers 722 – sped into view. It shot past in a cloud of dust. The great Stirling Moss and his co-driver, Denis Jenkinson, hurtled on through Italy in their Mercedes-Benz 300SLR, heading for victory in the 1955 Mille Miglia. The boy headed home to the nearby town of Lucca with a heavy heart. He and his family were emigrating to America and would be leaving within weeks. Soon, he would be crossing the Atlantic on a ship that he believed would be carrying him away from the allure of motor racing for ever. But, for 15-year-old Mario Andretti, that could hardly have been further from the truth.

Nothing could offer a more graphic illustration of the great American dream than the life lived by Mario.

Born near Trieste, in the early months of the Second World War, he spent the first seven years of his life in a refugee camp. His racing hero had been the Italian double World Champion, Alberto Ascari, who was killed at Monza almost as the Andretti family set foot on American soil in the spring of 1955. Once in the USA, Mario and his twin brother, Aldo, pulled out all the stops in an effort to become involved in racing.

Eventually, the pair of them scrimped and saved enough to buy a 1948 Hudson. In his fourth race, Aldo flipped the car so spectacularly that he ended up hospitalised, and in a coma for a week. A terrified Mario apparently told his parents that his brother had fallen off a truck while watching him race and been knocked out. Legend has it that when Aldo woke up, he said to his brother: 'I'm sure glad that you were the one who had to tell Dad!'

Mario Andretti drove for Ferrari on a part-time basis during the 1971-72 seasons.

Opposite page
Living the American dream: Andretti became a Champion in both Formula 1 and Indycar.

MARIO ANDRETTI

The hard-charging American was a popular and charismatic addition to the Formula 1 paddock.

With Team Lotus teammate Gunnar Nilsson *(on right)* and Lotus engineer Tony Southgate *(left)* in 1977. Nilsson was diagnosed with cancer the following season and died later that year.

In 1964 Mario had his first outing on the notorious Langhorne oval dirt track. Driving the 'Windmill Truckers' Special' prepared by the legendary Tommy Hinnershitz, the team's Chief Mechanic, he was lapped five times by race winner, A J Foyt. Mario was on his way. He quickly graduated to the elegant Dean Van Lines Special, one of the Watson-Offy front-engined roadsters so characteristic of the period. Clint Brawner, for whom Mario would eventually post his sole Indy 500 victory, entered this machine.

In 1965 he qualified fourth, and finished third, at Indianapolis to win the Rookie of the Year award, while the following year he notched up the first of two consecutive pole positions at The Brickyard. Two years later, his superb versatility was underlined by victories in both the Daytona 500 NASCAR classic and the Sebring 12-hour sports car race. It was, there-fore, not totally surprising that the Team Lotus boss, Colin Chapman – still reeling from the death of Jim Clark – should seek to give Andretti a try at the wheel of a Grand Prix machine.

Armed with the splendid Lotus 49B, Mario started the 1968 US Grand Prix at Watkins Glen from pole position. He led initially, but then Jackie Stewart's Matra went by, leaving Andretti to retire while running second. In 1969 he was signed to drive for Lotus on a restricted basis – as and when his American racing commitments permitted.

He was also linked with Lotus on the American racing scene. Throughout the month of May, at Indianapolis, he set the pace in the four-wheel-drive Lotus 64, only for a hub failure to pitch him into the wall. The accident left distinctive flash burns on both cheeks, just below his goggle line. Undaunted, he climbed into Brawner's spare Hawk and won the race going away. Later that season the four-wheel-drive Lotus 63 would give him a similar fright, when he crashed heavily on the first lap of the German Grand Prix. Once again, Mario walked away from the wreck. The man was made from tough stuff.

Unquestionably Andretti was Formula 1 material, yet while he loved the world of European open-wheelers, there was never any way in which he would abandon Indycars. The next six seasons would see him lead a hectic life as he divided his time between these two loves, jetting back and forth across the Atlantic sometimes as often as a couple of times each week, in the height of the season.

'In the early 1970s,' he later remembered. 'I was really torn between leaving Indycar racing and concentrating on Formula 1. I recall saying to Peter Revson that I envied the hell out of him. He was doing just a couple of 500-milers in the States each year, and spending the rest of his time with McLaren in Formula 1. It was exactly the programme I wanted.

'There isn't much security in this business, but my Firestone tyre contracted represented a lot of that for me. I dropped Formula 1 pretty much from 1973–74. I had run for Ferrari the two previous years, but they quit Firestone at the end of 1972 – as did Lotus. They didn't really need me in Formula 1. because they had their own guys in Europe.' Yet he was a popular addition to the Grand Prix scene on a personal level. When Andretti walks into a room, you are conscious that here is someone with great charisma. He is civil and articulate, and has always radiated star quality – underpinned by a firm sense of values.

At the end of the 1974 season he returned to Formula 1, driving the new Parnelli VPJ4. The car was named after the 1963 Indy 500 winner, Parnelli Jones, who, together with fellow racer Vel Miletich, had established the Vel's Parnelli Indycar Team. Now Parnelli recruited British engineer Maurice Phillippe to design him a brand new Grand Prix challenger, and Andretti was signed up as the driver.

Initial signs were promising. It qualified third for its debut outing in the US Grand Prix, but never really followed that up with worthwhile performances during the following year, 1975. Parnelli never quite got behind it, and the project ran out of steam – and sponsorship – after the 1976 Long Beach Grand Prix. If nothing else, the demise of the team served as a reminder that the uncompromising Andretti edge, seen so often in wheel-to-wheel track situations, could also translate to business dealings. Mario was

International Trophy race at Silverstone, 1978: six victories in the formidable Lotus 79 secured the World Championship.

furious that he had been misled by their apparent commitment to do the whole season, complaining that Parnelli 'put him out on the street' after Long Beach. He refused to have anything more to do with them, and withdrew from their American racing programme as well. Nobody took Mario Andretti for granted.

He had been loaned to Lotus for the first race of the 1976 season, but quickly decided that the latest, ultra-twitchy Type 77 was not up his street. In that race – the Brazilian Grand Prix – he had collided with team-mate Ronnie Peterson. After Parnelli's withdrawal Mario then started casting around for possible fresh alternatives. He accepted an offer from Frank Williams to drive the Wolf-Williams in the International Trophy at Silverstone, during which Gunnar Nilsson blew past him in the now heavily-revised Lotus. Mario was impressed. He got together with Colin Chapman and they soon forged a deal.

Chapman had effectively decided to start at technical base camp, from which he would evolve a whole new concept of Formula 1 car design. Many of

these aerodynamic developments were tried on the Lotus 77, and Mario ended up by winning the 1976 Japanese Grand Prix at Fuji – the race at which James Hunt clinched his World Championship. In 1977 Chapman unveiled the revolutionary Lotus 78 'wing car', which literally sucked itself to the road by means of inverted aerofoil-shaped side pods. This was Lotus' 'something for nothing' car, and Mario relished the challenge of developing it. He and Chapman worked well together, striking up a sympathetic and communicative partnership. Mario was prepared to spare no efforts in order to get the best out of the new car and the Lotus chief appreciated that.

Mario should have won the 1977 World Championship, but a spate of engine failures intervened to thwart those ambitions. He had agreed to stay with Lotus for 1978, but then Ferrari appeared and offered to double whatever Chapman had offered in an attempt to recruit the American as Niki Lauda's successor. Andretti was absolutely straight with Chapman, who proved sufficiently shrewd to match Ferrari's offer without complaint. Neither really

Opposite and below
Andretti and Team Lotus boss Colin Chapman were the most potent force in Formula 1 during the 1977–78 seasons.

wanted to fracture their partnership, but Colin could see his driver's viewpoint.

There was another side to this, of course. In order to fund part of Andretti's pay rise, Chapman signed Ronnie Peterson as his second driver for 1978. The blond Swede's was recognised as one of the very quickest men in the business, but his career had been in the doldrums for several seasons and he now jumped at the chance to revive it. Peterson also came for virtually nothing. His salary was paid by sponsorship from well-known racing philanthropist Count 'Googhie' Zanon, and commercial backer Polar Caravans.

Chapman took the wing car concept another step down the line for 1978, developing the Lotus 79 ground-effect car. 'If it hugged the road any closer, it would be a white line,' said an impressed Andretti after his first drive. Clearly it was in another league compared with most of the opposition, and Mario's precise and measured driving style capitalised on the car's handling advantage to brilliant effect. He won the Belgian, Spanish, French, German and Dutch Grands Prix with the Lotus 79 – in addition to the season opener in Argentina which he bagged at the wheel of the early Type 78. Peterson proved to be every bit as quick as his team-mate, but stuck by his deal to play second fiddle. 'The Lotus 78 is the car it is largely because of the development effort put in by

Mario,' said the Swede. The two men quickly became close friends.

Yet the season's domination ended on a tragic note. A multiple pile-up at the start of the Italian Grand Prix left Peterson with broken legs. Despite initial assurances that he would make a complete recovery, he died in the small hours of the following morning. Mario was bereft. 'Motor racing is, tragically, also this,' was all he could say to the scrum of news reporters as he left Milan's Niguarda clinic, where Peterson had succumbed.

By this stage in his career, Andretti had won a total of 12 Grands Prix. At the height of his championship success it was almost inconceivable that he would not win another. Yet that was to be the case. In 1979 Lotus lost its short-term performance advantage as rival teams – notably Williams – built better and more competitive ground-effect racers. In 1981 he switched to Alfa Romeo, and then dropped out of full-time Formula 1. He had a fruitless outing for Williams at Long Beach the following year, followed by a glorious return to Ferrari for the Italian Grand Prix in the wake of the tragic death of Gilles Villeneuve and the hospitalisation of Didier Pironi. The 'Old Boy' as he was now affectionately referred to by many of his colleagues, planted the Ferrari 126C2 turbo on pole position and finished a storming third.

Andretti did the bulk of the development work on the 'ground-effect' Lotus 79, establishing his right as lead driver over Ronnie Peterson during their dominant 1978 Championship year.

As the other teams caught up so Lotus found itself off the pace during 1979-80.

Rose-tinted spectacles? A final, unsuccessful, full season in Formula 1 with Alfa Romeo in 1981 prompted a return to the US racing scene.

After a final, disappointing, Formula 1 outing for the Prancing Horse at Las Vegas, Mario called time on his Grand Prix career. He was 42 years old, but there was still plenty of racing left under his belt and he would continue to compete on the Indycar scene for over a decade. He won his final Indycar race in the Newman Haas team's Lola-Ford on the short oval track at Phoenix, Arizona, in 1993 and also qualified at a sensational 234mph average to take pole position on the Michigan super speedway that same year. Not bad for a fellow of 53!

In the last years of his career, Mario gained enormous satisfaction from watching the racing progress of his elder son, Michael, who developed into a formidable Indycar competitor during the 1980s. Yet son or not, when the chips were down Mario regarded him as just another competitor. On the final lap Portland Indycar race in 1986, Michael was limping, with a misfiring engine, up the final straight to the chequered flag when Dad came zooming out of the final corner to pip him at the post and take the win. Michael later hinted that it might have been nice if Mario had let him stay ahead. Mario fixed his son with a stare. 'That's not the way it works, Michael,' he said quietly. A Racer indeed, to the very core of his soul.

Piers Courage

HE FAILED TO WIN EVEN ONE OF THE 28 GRANDS Prix during his career, but many believe that Piers Raymond Courage was on the verge of greatness when he was killed in the 1970 Dutch Grand Prix at Zandvoort. He was driving a de Tomaso for his friend Frank Williams at the time, and the horrendous, fiery accident which cost his life made a deep and lasting impression in the minds of his colleagues, even at a time when deaths in motor racing were commonplace.

Piers was born into the famous English brewing dynasty in 1941. He was educated at Eton, where he became a close friend of Sheridan Thynne (Thynne himself would later become Commercial Director of Williams). The Courage family farmed in rural Essex, and intended that their son should qualify as an accountant. However, when he was just 16 years old Piers borrowed a copy of Rex Hayes's book, *The Vanishing Litres*, and, from that point on, his young mind was captivated by images of huge green Bentleys thundering down the Mulsanne straight at Le Mans. His desire to become a racing driver under-standably met with acute disapproval from his parents. But despite their concern he bought a Lotus Seven on his 20th birthday, which he built up from a kit of parts. That little sports car represented the launching pad for his lofty ambitions.

Courage overcame an early tendency to fly off the road to gain his Formula 1 maturity. In a Parnell BRM at Monza in 1968 *(left)* and finishing second at Monaco the following year in the Frank Williams-owned Brabham *(above)*.

Opposite page
Eton-educated Courage went against his family's wishes to pursue a career in motor racing.

Second place at
Monaco with the
Williams Brabham
in 1969 proved that
he had the talent
to win races.

He also shone at Monza,
eventually finishing in
fifth place.

Progressively, Piers traded up to a Formula 3 single seater, and abandoned his accountancy studies for good. 'That decision didn't exactly switch off the family funds,' recalled Sheridan Thynne. 'But it certainly reduced them from a stream to a trickle.' Nevertheless, young Courage was now hell-bent on becoming a racing driver. He never looked back.

He quickly gained a reputation as one of the country's top Formula 3 stars during 1965, driving a private Brabham for his pal, Charles Lucas. He had more-or-less tamed an early tendency for flying off the road and, for 1966 was offered a drive with the works supported Lotus Formula 3 team. The downside of this deal was that the Lotus 41 he had to drive was not generally regarded to be as driver-friendly as the rival Brabhams. By this time, he was engaged to Lady Sarah Maguerite Curzon, daughter of the pre-war motor racing pioneer, Earl Howe. Throughout the 1966 season Courage raced well, but still proved worry-ingly prone to coming unstuck.

'Piers was inconsistent,' remembers Charles Lucas. 'Sometimes he drove like a dream, sometimes he flew off into the trees for no apparent reason. In 1967, when he was paired with Chris Irwin at BRM, Piers got too twitchy and went over the top.' Courage and Irwin, old Formula 3 sparring partners, had been recruited by the top-line BRM team to be tutored as

stars of the future. Irwin certainly looked more convincing, and got the lion's share of the guest drives after Piers blotted his copybook by crashing at Monaco. He also drove a Formula 2 McLaren for Guildford garage owner John Coombs, a longtime private entrant. Coombs began to get so concerned over the sequence of accidents that he begged Piers to retire. 'Otherwise you'll kill yourself, I know you will,' he said.

One man who had total faith in Courage was Frank Williams. Having scrimped and scraped his way into motor racing during the early 1960s, Williams had started a second-hand racing car business in 1967. He also became an agent for Brabham racing cars, and began his partnership with Piers by fielding him in a new Brabham BT21B Formula 3 car in the prestigious Motor Show 200 meeting at Brands Hatch.

It was the start of a great partnership which would see them move into Formula 2 the following year, and then into Formula 1 when – in 1969 – Williams bought an ex-works Brabham BT26. More than two decades later, listening to Frank talk, it was quite clear that he still regarded his long-lost friend as someone very special:

'As a character, there seriously has not been anybody like him in motor racing since,' said Williams. 'He wasn't an aristocrat, but he came from a

Monaco, 1970. The all-new de Tomaso was something of an unknown quantity. Courage and team owner Frank Williams struggled at first.

very privileged family. He went to Eton, and lived among a group of friends like Sheridan, who were different to the average geezer that I was accustomed to. He also lived a very social life in London, married to Sally – who really did come from an aristrocratic background.'

After a promising Formula 2 season in 1968, Piers went off to race in the Tasman series with the McLaren M4A he had purchased from John Coombs. He was clearly something of a reformed character, having finally learned how to run along the narrow line between unbridled speed and over-zealous enthusiasm. Now he was not only quick, but supremely reliable too, and rounded off that winter tour with a brilliant win in the streaming rain on the demanding road circuit at Longford, in Tasmania. Then it was back to Europe for the start of the Formula 1 Championship in the newly-acquired Williams Brabham-Ford. During the course of the season Piers netted two superb second places, at Monaco and in the US Grand Prix at Watkins Glen.

'His performance at the Glen was tremendous,' recalled Frank. 'It absolutely knocked me out. He was running third between the works Brabhams of Jacky Ickx and Jack Brabham himself, and the way he kept Jack behind – hurling stones all over the man whose company had built our car in the first place – was absolutely terrific.

'Ickx eventually retired, so Piers had a clear run to second place in the closing stages. Many people watching reported that this was one of the few occasions they had seen Jack Brabham in a black fury at the end of the race.'

Yet it was Courage's drive in the Italian Grand Prix, at Monza, which really cemented his position as a front line Formula 1 driver. For much of the race he was embroiled in a furious battle for the lead, which eventually saw Jackie Stewart's Matra win by inches from Jochen Rindt's Lotus, to post a win which clinched the Scot's first World Championship.

'To my mind, that was the day Piers came of age as a Grand Prix driver,' said Stewart. 'Up to that point, I had always been a little concerned about his unpredictability in close traffic. But he ran with the leading bunch – Rindt, Bruce McLaren, Jean-Pierre Beltoise and me – for many laps and I never had a moment's worry. He was driving immaculately and always with total discipline.'

For 1970 Frank Williams took what he hoped would be a step up the Grand Prix ladder, by securing a deal to run a brand new car built by the Italian de Tomaso company. The deal was that de Tomaso would provide the cars, and Frank the engines, backing and team support. By this stage, Piers was being romanced by Ferrari as a possible partner to Jacky Ickx in 1970. The offer was a massive £30,000, but Piers wanted to remain with Frank. He stayed driving for his friend on a nominal £3,000 retainer, which he topped up with another £22,500 pounds by signing to drive sports cars for Alfa Romeo.

'Because of his personality as an individual, rather than as a racing driver, Piers found the concept of achieving success with Frank enormously appealing,' said Thynne. 'It was a case of Frank and Piers wanting to show Ferrari and Lotus that they could get the job done. He had become very mature, and was strongly

Courage rejected an offer to drive for Ferrari in order to stay with Williams in 1970. He enjoyed the notion of beating the Formula 1 establishment with a new team.

motivated to stay with Frank and have things continue as they had done in the past.'

The season began on a difficult note. The de Tomaso was not competitive, and Piers had to manhandle the car in order to produce any semblance of competitive form. Yet there was a promising moment when he finished third in the International Trophy race at Silverstone. But he retired in South Africa and Belgium, failed to start in Spain and was not classified – despite still running at the finish – in Monaco.

Yet it was all pulled apart with a terrible abruptness. Picking up places as he moved up the field at

Zandvoort, Piers crashed and perished as the de Tomaso was consumed by fire.

'I was heartbroken,' recalled Williams. 'I worshipped the guy. He was totally adorable. He had terrific car control and skill, and was extremely intelligent – always thinking about ways to enhance the performance of any car he was driving'

Lady Sarah has the last word. 'They were such happy times, and everybody had such incredible optimism – even when things weren't going right,' she said. 'Piers stayed with Frank because the chemistry was there.'

Promise unfulfilled: Courage at Jarama – practising for the Spanish Grand Prix – in 1970, the year he was killed.

François Cevert

FRANÇOIS CEVERT WAS A DAZZLING PERSONALITY; every inch the Grand Prix driver. The son of a Paris jeweller, his technique behind the wheel was spiced with a dash of extrovert brio. Yet he had matured into one of the most accomplished drivers in Formula 1 when he was killed during practice for the United States Grand Prix, at Watkins Glen, in 1973.

Cevert laid the foundations of his professional career at the wheel of a Formula 3 Tecno, in which he won the French national championship in 1968. The following year he graduated into Formula 2, still with Tecno, and won the last international Formula 2 race to be held on the famous Reims road circuit. But his big chance came mid-way through 1970, when Tyrrell driver Johnny Servoz-Gavin abruptly decided to retire from Formula 1 after crashing during practice for the Monaco Grand Prix.

Having consulted with his team leader, Jackie Stewart, Ken Tyrrell opted to sign Cevert purely on the basis of his evident talent and not – as was

The dashing François Cevert in 1971, the year of his first – and only – Grand Prix victory.

speculated at the time – as a result of pressure from his key sponsor, the French ELF petroleum company.

Cevert drove with considerable confidence from the moment he first took his seat in the Tyrrell team's March 701. His best drive came at the Canadian Grand Prix, where he worked his way through to fourth place before being delayed by a broken rear suspension damper. During the latter part of the season Stewart had his hands full developing the new Tyrrell 001 prototype, which the team had produced in conditions of strict secrecy. So when Cevert joined the team he had to manage with one of the old March 701s, scoring just a single point at Monza, until 1971, when he was able to get into his stride at the wheel of a car identical to that driven by Jackie.

The relationship between the two Tyrrell drivers was remarkably close and collaborative. For his part, Jackie had the confidence to know where he stood in

the Formula 1 pecking order, and he was always prepared to pass on his knowledge to younger drivers. He quickly came to admire Cevert's energy and enthusiasm, and recognised that he had a genuine talent that needed to be coaxed and nurtured. François proved to be a willing pupil. He stood in awe of Jackie, and listened carefully to the man who had become his mentor and inspiration.

The 1971 German Grand Prix, at the Nürburgring, was possibly the first tangible indication of François's burgeoning talent. He finished in second place, just thirty seconds behind Jackie, after 170 miles of racing around the tortuous 14-mile circuit. And to round it off, Cevert posted the fastest race lap: only one second away from Stewart's pole position time.

It was now quite clear that Cevert had established himself as a formidable driver who was quite capable of supporting Stewart at the front of the field.

The 1972 season was a difficult one for reigning Champions Tyrrell, but Cevert's reputation as a future World Champion continued to grow.

FRANÇOIS CEVERT

Cevert was being
groomed for the
number one spot at
Tyrrell after Jackie
Stewart's retirement.

In the spare Tyrell 004
during practice for
the 1972 German
Grand Prix.

For the Italian Grand Prix, Stewart found himself hobbled with an overheating transmission. He qualified behind Cevert, leaving him to get firmly entrenched in the battle for the lead. The 1971 race was the final 'slipstream special' to be held at Monza. The cars circulated in a closely-bunched 150mph swarm, as they ran virtually flat-out from start to finish. In subsequent years, the circuit would be broken up by tight chicanes – ostensibly on safety grounds. But this was an epic confrontation, and Cevert oh-so-nearly triumphed.

He looked set to win, only to find himself outfumbled by Peter Gethin's BRM P160 and Ronnie Peterson's March 711 on the final, frenzied sprint to the flag. Cevert driver finished third, barely one-tenth of a second behind the winning BRM.

It only seemed a matter of time before François would win a race for Tyrrell, and a timely slice of luck duly came the Frenchman's way in that year's United States Grand Prix at Watkins Glen. Jackie qualified on pole and led the early stages of the race from Denny Hulme's McLaren and Cevert. It was not long before François displaced the McLaren and fell into formation behind his team-mate. But this Tyrrell 1–2 was not destined to last for long.

Stewart was suffering badly from a lack of tyre grip. He eventually dropped away, to finish a frustrated fifth, and left François to win the final race of the year and bag a $50,000 prize. Stewart had long since clinched the World Championship, but this splendid win vaulted Cevert into third place in the final table.

For the 1972 season, Tyrrell designer Derek Gardner produced a completely new car, much lighter and more manoeuvrable. 'Something which Jackie could make the most of,' he concluded. The short-chassis Tyrrell 005/006 range proved ultimately quicker than its predecessor, although slightly more nervous and sensitive. While it took a driver of

Six second places in 1973, including this one at Montjuich Park, established Cevert as a regular front-runner in Formula 1.

One for the ladies: Cevert fitted the image of the glamorous Grand Prix star.

Stewart's calibre to maximise the new car's potential, the fact that Cevert usually ran the Scot very close was an indication of just how quickly the team's second driver was progressing.

Taken as a whole, the 1972 Championship programme proved a disappointment for Tyrrell. The new car was only introduced mid-season, and Jackie was forced to miss one race while recuperating from the effects of a duodenal ulcer. Add to that the fact that Emerson Fittipaldi and the Lotus 72 was generally a more competitive pairing, and it was perhaps no surprise that Stewart and Cevert could only manage second and sixth respectively in that season's Championship.

The 1973 season opened with François performing superbly in the Argentine Grand Prix at Buenos Aires. He was leading in the closing stages, only to be outbraked decisively by Fittipaldi's Lotus with just seven laps to run. Second places would also come Cevert's way in the Spanish, French, Dutch and German Grands Prix. The last two results saw him right on Stewart's tail at the chequered flag. Fourth place in the Italian Grand Prix clinched Jackie's third World

Championship – his last – before the team embarked on its North American tour.

The Canadian Grand Prix, at Mosport Park, turned into a lap charting fiasco, with the final result in doubt for several hours after the end of the race. Not that this concerned François. He had been involved in a tangle with Jody Scheckter's McLaren, as a result of which the Frenchman slammed head-on into a barrier at around 100mph. 'I am alive today because my Tyrrell is so strong,' François told his mother on the telephone from Niagara Falls, where he had stopped off *en route* to the United States Grand Prix, the final race of the season.

'By this stage in his career, François was really driving on top form,' said Jo Ramirez, then a Tyrrell mechanic. 'He was a lovely guy, and everybody in the team really had a lot of time for him. He had huge potential.'

Despite driving with strapped-up ankles, Cevert was right on the pace as qualifying at the Glen drew to a close. Fourth fastest, he was determined to gain pole position as he went out for one final run. Then he failed to appear. An ominous hush fell over the circuit. Cars trickled into the pits and their engines were stilled.

Streaking into the tricky uphill esses, François had seemed to be slightly off-line; his Tyrrell clipped the left-hand side of the track. It bounced back across the tarmac and punched an 130mph hole in the double-height Armco on the opposite side of the road. The horrifying impact ripped the car asunder.

Cevert was killed instantly, on the circuit where he had won his sole Grand Prix victory. The Tyrrell team, shattered by what had happened, withdrew from the race and prepared for the long trip home.

Riding high at Jarama in 1972: his death at Watkins Glen, during practice for the 1973 US Grand Prix, robbed the sport of a genuine talent.

Emerson Fittipaldi

Emerson Fittipaldi was crowned the youngest-ever Formula 1 World Champion in 1972. He was just 25.

EMERSON FITTIPALDI LAID THE FOUNDATIONS of Brazil's passion for Grand Prix racing which has endured, and prospered, ever since the young lad from São Paulo won the 1970 United States Grand Prix – only his fourth-ever Formula 1 race – at the wheel of a Lotus 72.

His father, Wilson senior, was one of Brazil's most respected motor racing journalists and broadcasters. He had come to Europe to report on the exploits of

fellow South Americans, Juan Manuel Fangio and Froilán González, back in the early 1950s. A passionate motor racing enthusiast, he had also raced saloon cars briefly during the immediate post-war years. Emerson and his elder brother, Wilson junior, both began racing karts at an early age. Emerson cut his car racing teeth in a Formula Vee, before arriving in Britain at the start of the 1969 season. He was 22. He acquired a Merlyn Formula Ford car and quickly became the man to beat on the British national scene.

No question about it, Emerson was seriously quick. He mastered Formula Ford in a matter of months and then moved on to dominate the British Formula 3 series with the sort of flair we would later associate with his compatriot, Ayrton Senna, over a decade later. He drove a semi-works Lotus and attracted the close scrutiny of Colin Chapman.

Never one to pass up the opportunity of recruiting a likely lad for the future, the Lotus boss signed Fittipaldi up for a full season of European Championship Formula 2, starting in 1970. Yet even before he had won his first race in that category, events were conspiring to hurry Emerson's rise up the ladder towards the Formula 1 break which, in truth, had almost seemed his right since he first stepped off the plane from Brazil.

In the aftermath of Piers Courage's death in the 1970 Dutch Grand Prix, Frank Williams had tried hard to secure Emerson's services for the balance of the season. But there was no way Chapman would permit this to happen. Fittipaldi was locked into the Lotus system with an exclusive contract, but the interest from Williams at least speeded Chapman's decision to give his new lad a Formula 1 try-out.

That opportunity came in the British Grand Prix at Brands Hatch. In addition to the two Lotus 72s fielded for Jochen Rindt and John Miles there was also an outdated 49C for the Brazilian kid. He finished a strong seventh, then went on to drive the same car to fourth place in the German Grand Prix at Hockenheim, bagging the first of many helpings of World Championship points.

The entire Lotus effort was knocked sideways when Rindt was killed practising for the Italian Grand Prix

As reigning Champion in 1973 he won three races but the title returned to Jackie Stewart, who had been Champion in 1971.

Fittipaldi established his potential early on, with a fine fourth place for Lotus at Hockenheim in 1970 – only his second Grand Prix.

Three full seasons with Team Lotus yielded nine victories in the Type 72, including this one at Jarama in 1972…

… and again at the Österreichring.

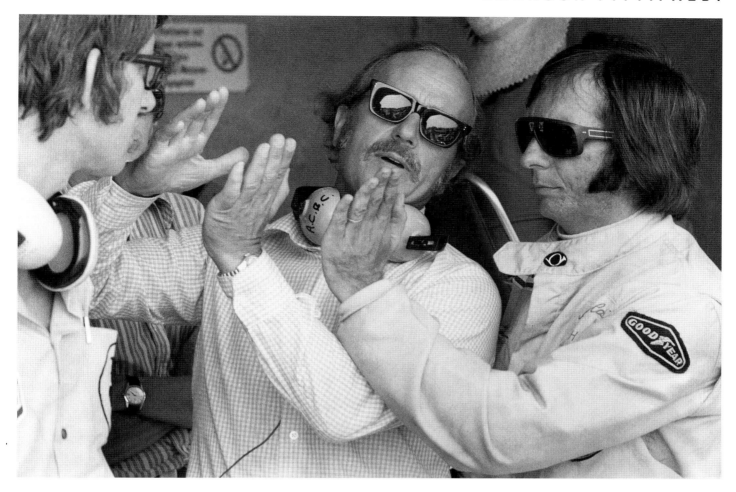

at Monza. John Miles, who had always been acutely apprehensive about the 72's potential constructional frailty, lost heart and left the team. Suddenly Emerson found himself propelled into the *de facto* team leadership and cemented this newly achieved status with a fortuitous victory at Watkins Glen.

Fittipaldi would lead the Lotus Formula 1 assault into the 1971 season, but Rindt's death had slowed the team's development momentum. Emerson was still learning the ropes and a mid-season road accident, which left him driving a couple of races with broken ribs, also conspired to undermine his efforts. At the end of the season he was sixth in the World Championship with best placings of second in Austria and third at Silverstone. It is also fair to say that the Lotus 72 needed further development although, despite this, the Brazilian driver commandingly outclassed his equally-inexperienced team-mate, the Swiss Reine Wisell.

Yet it was clear to Colin Chapman that Fittipaldi was developing into an intuitive racer. He was easy on the equipment, very perceptive when it came to developing the car and blindingly quick when he needed to be. Further development saw the Lotus 72 emerging as the car to beat in 1972 when Emerson

romped to the World Championship, and became the sport's youngest-ever title holder. In doing so he won the Spanish, Belgian, British, Austrian and Italian Grands Prix.

One of his most notable successes came in the British race at Brands Hatch where Emerson expertly paced himself in the closing stages to fend off a dramatic challenge by Jackie Stewart's Tyrrell. Sure enough, the Lotus was the superior car over the bumps, but Fittipaldi deployed its potential with just the right balance of forcefulness and restraint. He was becoming quite an operator.

Fittipaldi's team-mate throughout the 1972 season was the gritty Australian Dave Walker, who had won the previous season's British Formula 3 title in a works Lotus. It seemed he was a logical choice to make the graduation to Formula 1, but he failed demonstrably to make the grade. Whether or not he was given parity of equipment in this team which had a notorious reputation for favouring its number one drivers is another matter altogether, but Chapman decided on a change of driver for 1973.

It was absolutely characteristic of the Lotus boss that he wanted to have his cake and eat it, which is precisely what he did by signing Ronnie Peterson to

Fittipaldi emerged as a superb development driver – as well as a racer – whose input proved invaluable to Lotus boss Colin Chapman during the early days of the Lotus 72.

Monza, 1972, where Fittipaldi secured his first World Championship. The arrival of Ronnie Peterson at Lotus in 1973 upset the balance within the team and prompted the Brazilian to look elsewhere for a drive in 1974.

drive alongside Fittipaldi. The Swede came with impressive credentials that didn't need explaining to Emerson. He knew all about Ronnie's talent from the days when they raced wheel-to-wheel in Formula Two. Welcoming him into his own personal enclave was a different matter altogether.

Emerson started the season briskly with victories in Argentina, Brazil and Spain. Grand Prix racing is a psychological sport and if that was meant to be a pre-emptive strike against the Swede, it simply wasn't going to work. There were signs that Fittipaldi was getting rattled, not least when he collided with the unusually brave McLaren novice Jody Scheckter, who proved difficult to dislodge from the lead in the French Grand Prix at Paul Ricard. Ironically, Emerson's slip opened the way for Peterson to post his maiden Formula 1 victory.

By the end of the 1973 season, Peterson had got the upper hand in terms of sheer speed, although Lotus insiders were still convinced that Emerson was the better technical operator. In essence, that was what got to the Brazilian. He would spend his qualifying sessions carefully finalising the optimum chassis settings while Ronnie meandered off on his own, getting more and more confused. With five minutes to go, Ronnie would say 'put Emerson's settings on my car' and go straight out to blitz the man who originated them.

Some shrewd lateral thinking may have convinced Fittipaldi that he was better off in another team where his technical input would not be handed on a plate to a colleague who would then use it to beat him. More likely, when the offer of a drive with McLaren landed on his mat, he was attracted by the substantial

retainer provided by title sponsors Marlboro and the fact that the team's M23 challenger was newer and more competitive than the old Lotus 72.

Either way, Emerson made the switch. It paid off handsomely with three more Grand Prix victories and a second World Championship. There were signs that Fittipaldi was taking a slightly more tactical and pragmatic approach to his racing, and this became even more evident in 1975 when his Ford-engined McLaren was outgunned by Niki Lauda's more powerful Ferrari. Emerson was as quick as ever. Indeed, he was driving so neatly that his M23 looked as though it was on rails for much of the time. But then he dropped a bombshell.

At the end of 1975 he announced that he was quitting the McLaren team to join the all-Brazilian Formula 1 operation that had been set up by his brother Wilson at the start of that year. Funded lavishly by Copersucar – the Brazilian sugar cartel – this decision effectively spelled the end of Emerson as a front-line Grand Prix driver.

At the age of 29 he had consigned himself to Grand Prix oblivion driving a series of generally uncompetitive racing cars for the next five years. Only a rousing second place behind Carlos Reutemann's Ferrari in the 1978 Brazilian Grand Prix at Rio de Janeiro fleetingly punctuated a depressing downward spiral. At the end of 1980, Emerson stood down from driving in favour of his young compatriot Chico Serra. The team struggled on through 1982 before the financial waters closed above their heads.

This, however, was far from the end of the story of Emerson Fittipaldi, racing driver. He first toyed with

The choice of McLaren proved a shrewd one: Fittipaldi, pictured with Teddy Mayer, won his second World Championship in his first season with the team.

63

Two years with McLaren saw the Brazilian operating at the peak of his powers, making his decision to join his brother, Wilson, in setting up the new Copersucar-Fittipaldi team all the more difficult to understand.

IMSA sports cars in the USA, then, after a two-year lay-off, started his CART single-seater career at the age of 38. He quickly proved that his finesse and judgement had not deserted him during those dark years. He had just the touch required to run on the high speed ovals and it was only appropriate that his first victory should come in the 1985 Michigan 500, when he beat Al Unser in a straight fight.

In 1989 he won the Indy 500 driving a private Penske for Pat Patrick's team. It was his fifth season with the team and this success represented the highlight of the season in which he won the CART Championship.

That Indy 500 victory was quite extraordinary. The veteran Brazilian found himself locked in a wheel-to-wheel with Al Unser's Lola and, with just two laps to go, Emerson dived inside his key rival and the two cars made light contact. It was just enough to send Al rattling into the outside wall, but instead of leaping from his cockpit to berate Fittipaldi – which one might have expected in Formula 1 – he stood by his wrecked car offering the thumbs-up signal with both hands as his rival cruised his cooling-off lap.

In 1990 Emerson joined the works Penske team, but had a generally disappointing season. The trend continued in 1991, but in 1992 he bounced back into

contention with four wins, then scored his second Indy 500 victory in 1993, the year in which Nigel Mansell very nearly conquered the Brickyard at his first attempt.

Ironically, it was at Michigan – the scene of his first CART victory – that the 49-year-old veteran had the accident in 1996 which signalled the start of his retirement. He was sidelined for three months after a horrifying 190mph accident at the oval circuit during which onlookers feared for his life as his Hogan Racing Penske-Mercedes slammed into the wall in a terrifying ripple of flame.

The Brazilian veteran underwent five hours of surgery in Miami to insert a titanium plate in his spine and a bone graft onto a damaged veterbra. His car snapped wildly out of control after clipping rookie Greg Moore's Reynard-Mercedes on the first lap of the Michigan 500. He also sustained a partially collapsed lung in the fiery impact.

Despite Fittipaldi's initial assertion that he hoped to continue racing, many Indycar observers correctly predicted that the accident would prompt Emerson to consider his future with a view to retiring at the end of the season. Yet he still couldn't quite officially bring himself to mouth the words 'I'm retiring.'

However, in 1997 he was involved in a microlight accident near his São Paulo home, the two-seater in which he and his young son were riding dropped – mercifully for them – into a swamp.

This dreadful impact aggravated his recently-healed back injury, but again he survived to make a full recovery. This time doctors said 'enough is enough', and Emerson was shrewd enough to know that the game was up. His fans across the world breathed a sigh of relief, happy that their hero would still be around for them to cheer him through a well-deserved retirement.

Plenty to think about. The Fittipaldi venture was not a success, although Emerson continued to drive for the team until the end of the 1980 season.

Niki Lauda

THE SLIGHTLY-BUILT, TRIPLE WORLD CHAMPION has transcended his brilliant achievements behind the wheel of a Grand Prix car to take a place in sporting history as a global hero. Born into a conservative Viennese family, whose wealth came from a string of paper processing plants, Lauda was seldom out of the limelight from the moment he got a toehold in Grand Prix racing in 1972.

A summary of his career includes borrowing £32,000 to buy a place in the March Grand Prix team, taking Ferrari back to the top with two World Championship titles in three years and nearly being burned alive in an accident during the 1976 German Grand Prix at the Nürburgring. Finally, he won his third World Championship after over two years in retirement; during that interval away from the cockpit he started his own airline, LaudaAir.

Lauda had a difficult time with the March 721G during his maiden Grand Prix season, 1972.

But it was his recovery from that potentially fatal accident, in 1976, that put Lauda on the map as somebody out of the ordinary. Despite receiving the Last Rites, he fought back to race again at Monza barely 10 weeks after death stared him in the face.

And there was more trauma to come, for in 1997 he successfully underwent a kidney transplant operation with an organ that had been donated by his younger brother, Florian.

But neither of these episodes come close to the anguish he experienced with the loss of a Lauda-air Boeing 767 over Thailand in 1992, a disaster that killed 223 people. The manner in which he described the emotions provoked by this tragedy directly mirrored the self-disciplined and analytical philosophy that he had applied to his own racing career: 'If I decide I want to race, drive into a guardrail and kill

myself, that is my own decision,' he said. 'But if you buy a ticket on my airline and you don't come back, it is totally different. Thank God the crash was basically down to the aeroplane itself and not to us. If LaudaAir had been shown to be responsible, I would have quit. It was the most profound experience of my life.'

Niki faced a great deal of parental opposition to his fledgling motor racing career. Having carved a promising path through Formula 2 in 1971, he found sponsorship from a Vienna bank that would pay the cost of his graduation into Formula 1. At this point Niki's grandfather, whom he never referred to as anyone but 'Old Lauda', pulled some strings behind the scenes and scuppered the deal. 'Young Lauda' was far from amused. Eventually, he got the money together by means of a complex deal, in which he mortgaged his own life against a loan from another bank. Unfortunately, the 1972 March 721 proved hopelessly uncompetitive and its successor, the 721G, was only marginally more promising.

Undaunted, Niki borrowed even more money in 1973 in order to secure a place in the BRM Formula 1 team. He calculated that his prize money earnings from BRM, together with his touring car contact with the Alpina BMW squad, would balance out the costs of the loan. He drove tremendously well in the rather outdated BRM P160, running third at Monaco,

Opportunity knocks: an offer to join Ferrari in 1974 was too good to ignore.

Five wins the following season secured the first of three World Championships.

Lauda's 1976
title defence was
derailed by the
Nürburgring accident.

Two years with Brabham
and the innovative
designer, Gordon Murray
(right) yielded just two
controversial wins.

second at Silverstone and scoring his first Championship points with a fifth place finish in Belgium. By the middle of the season, he had proved himself to be consistently the quickest of the BRM drivers and the team boss, Louis Stanley, agreed to shelve any further payments from him in exchange for his signing a contract for 1974 and 1975. Then came an offer from Ferrari that Niki knew he could not afford to pass up. Some hard legal negotiations got him off the hook with BRM and he was free, continuing onwards and upwards.

Niki's move to Maranello catapulted him into a new motor racing dimension. By 1974, Ferrari was in a different league to BRM. Although the Italian team had suffered a disappointing couple of years it looked to be on an upward curve, thanks to the management of the ambitious Luca di Montezemolo. He and Niki were like peas out of the same pod.

The Austrian matured as a driver in leaps and bounds throughout 1974. He won the Spanish and Dutch Grands Prix in commanding style and was prevented from winning more by a combination of inexperience and misfortune. Even so, he remained in with a shout of the World Championship right to the end, laying the groundwork for what would prove to be an outstanding 1975 season. By the start of the year, Lauda's meticulous driving style had been honed to a high level of excellence. His genius was to let the car do the work, applying an economy of style that was as unpretentious as it was effective. Harnessing the fine handling qualities of the new Ferrari 312T – which had a radical transverse gearbox transmitting the power from its flat-12 engine – Niki set the tone for the season by narrowly beating Emerson Fittipaldi's McLaren to win the Silverstone International Trophy.

His first Championship win of the season came at Monaco, followed by the Belgian, French and Spanish Grands Prix. After that it seemed that his title challenge was briefly derailed. James Hunt's Hesketh beat him into second place in a memorable Dutch Grand Prix at Zandvoort, and the British race was rendered chaotic by a sudden thunderstorm. Niki wound up eighth, and out of the points. A punctured tyre dropped him to third at the Nürburgring. Then he was sixth, hobbled by the wrong chassis settings, in a wet race at the Österreichring. Despite these setbacks his third place at Monza – where team-mate Clay Regazzoni won – was enough to clinch his first Championship, and he rounded off with his fifth win of the season in the US race at Watkins Glen.

At the start of 1976 it seemed as though Niki's run of success would swing seamlessly into the new season. He opened with wins in Brazil and South Africa in the 1975 spec 312T, then finished second to a hard-charging Regazzoni in the inaugural Long

Lauda's return to
Formula 1 in 1982,
with McLaren, saw
him return to the top
step of the podium in
only his third race – at
Long Beach, California.

Opposite page
**Parmalat man:
few drivers have
combined natural
speed and tactical
cunning with such
effectiveness as
Niki Lauda.**

**The brilliant McLaren
MP4/2 secured the
World Championship for
Lauda for a third
time in 1984.**

Beach street race in California. For the fourth round of the year – the Spanish Grand Prix – a revised T2 version of the car was readied, but Niki had recently been hospitalised, with two cracked ribs, following an accident at his home near Salzburg. Come the race itself, the Austrian was beaten by James Hunt. But when the McLaren was disqualified for a technical infringement, Niki was gifted the win. It was the start of an intense season-long rivalry between Lauda and his friend Hunt.

Even so, it looked as though Lauda would maintain the upper hand. He won in Monaco and Belgium, and finished third in Sweden. Hunt won at Paul Ricard, after the Ferrari suffered engine failure, but then the real controversy started. Hunt had beaten Lauda convincingly at Brands Hatch to win the British Grand Prix, but the Italian team protested the victory. Hunt, they alleged, had not been running when the race was

stopped following the multiple pile-up at Paddock Bend. He was, they contended, therefore ineligible to take the restart. The officials, apparently caving in to the demands of a partisan, vociferous crowd, had allowed him to start. The matter was eventually referred to an FIA Court of Appeal, to resurface later in the season.

Then came the Nürburgring, and all the wrangling was forgotten for the time being. Having started with rain tyres on a drying track, Niki came into the pits at the end of the first 14-mile lap. The Ferrari was switched to slicks, and Lauda was making up ground on the leaders as he plunged down through the pine forests over Adenau and began the long climb back up towards the main straight. Approaching the Bergwerk right hander, his car snapped out of control, slammed through the catch fencing on the right hand side of the circuit and crashed into a rock face. It bounced

Smiling again:
the Austrian's return
to Formula 1 saw his
competitive flame
rekindled.

back into the middle of the road, burst into flames, and was then hit by the Surtees of the American driver, Brett Lunger. The impact wrenched Lauda's helmet off, and it was only through the selfless efforts of fellow drivers Guy Edwards, Lunger, Arturo Merzario and a quick-witted marshal that Niki was rescued from the inferno.

For several days his life hung by a thread. Toxic fumes inhaled from the Ferrari's burning glassfibre bodywork had threatened his survival. His head and face were badly burned. Yet, incredibly, he would return to the cockpit for the Italian Grand Prix at Monza, having missed only three races. His head swathed in bandages through which the blood from his partially healed wounds continued to seep, Niki finished fourth and twice set fastest lap during the race. This was heroism and single-mindedness of epic proportions, but Lauda never looked on himself as a particularly brave man. He had a job that he wanted to do and that was sufficient motivation. The physical scars, which he bears to this day, never bothered him in the least. Or if they did, he never showed it.

Hunt certainly benefited from Lauda's absences, but the books were balanced when the FIA eventually deprived James of that controversial Brands Hatch win. The disqualification simply motivated the Englishman to go for broke, which he did with magnificent wins in Mosport Park and Watkins Glen. Finally, he clinched the title by a single point with a

third place finish on a soaking Mount Fuji circuit in Japan, a race from which Lauda had pulled out after two laps, deeming the conditions impossible.

'Niki Lauda is the bravest man I have ever known,' said James, in a tribute to his old friend. And he meant it. But such compliments did not prevent the partisan Italian press from railing at Lauda for apparently throwing away the Championship. Despite the insults, he stayed with the team and regained his Championship in 1977. Then he left, and joined the Bernie Ecclestone-owned Brabham-Alfa team.

He scored just two wins for his new team, one of which was a controversial success in Sweden with the BT46 'fan car' – the brainchild of the team's innovative designer, Gordon Murray. The BT46 used a gearbox driven fan to suck air from beneath the wide flat-12 engine in an effort to match the aerodynamic downforce generated by the sensational Lotus 79. This technical solution was eventually outlawed, but not before Niki had added another win to his tally, at Monza, the race that claimed the life of his friend and former team-mate, Ronnie Peterson.

Alfa Romeo produced an all-new engine for 1979, but its performance proved patchy and inconsistent. Niki could feel himself losing interest. Mid-way through qualifying at Montreal, he pulled into the pits and announced to Bernie Ecclestone that he wanted to retire. Bernie agreed that it was best if he quit on the spot. 'I was no longer getting any pleasure from driving round and round in circles,' he admitted. 'I feel I have better things to do with my life.'

His sabbatical lasted just over two seasons. Sensing he might be ready to revive his Formula 1 reputation, McLaren International chief Ron Dennis demonstrated considerable perspicacity by inviting him to test one of his team's cars at Donington Park. The new John Barnard-designed McLaren MP4/1 was very different to the old Brabham-Alfa, but Niki was hooked. As always, pragmatism ruled. 'Once I had made the decision to come back, the rest was easy,' he insisted disarmingly. 'OK, so I had a few fleeting doubts when I did that Donington test but, by the end of the day I reckoned I could do it.'

Dennis shrewdly included a clause in Niki's contract for 1982 that allowed him to replace the Austrian if he hadn't proved competitive within four races. Lauda duly obliged by winning at Long Beach, his third race of the season, and all was well. He won again at Brands Hatch in front of a particularly appreciative crowd. The English fans always rated Niki as a great favourite. There were no wins in 1983, but McLaren's new Porsche-built TAG turbo engine came on line towards the end of the year, proving instantly competitive.

It was clear that Lauda and his new team-mate, Alain Prost (who had replaced John Watson at the end of 1983), were going to be formidably competitive in 1984. And thus unfolded Niki's third World Championship season. Prost was quicker, particularly in qualifying, but Niki kept his nerve. Alain won seven races; Niki five. But the Austrian emerged on top by the wafer thin margin of half a point. 'Next year,' Niki assured Prost on the rostrum at the final race of the season. 'You will be Champion.'

He drove another year before retiring, winning his final Grand Prix at Zandvoort in 1985, where he fended off Prost in a no-holds-barred scrap that went right down to the wire. Prost took the Championship,

and Lauda bowed out after a relatively disappointing year. But his comeback had certainly proved the depth of his competitiveness and determination. Second time round, Niki Lauda was just as single-minded as he had been during those early years with BRM and Ferrari. As his contemporary Keke Rosberg, the 1982 World Champion for Williams, observed: 'Once or twice during 1984 I got into a wheel-to-wheel situation with Niki. He was very proper and correct – but totally unyielding. It was clear that if I didn't give way, then something would happen.' And Keke gave way.

Kyalami, 1979. A frustrating season with the Brabham-Alfa led to Lauda's retirement – for the first time. 'I was no longer getting any pleasure from driving round and round in circles,' he said.

Ronnie Peterson

MIKE HAILWOOD CALLED HIM 'MAD RONALD'. His mechanics, during his formative years with the March team, nicknamed him 'SuperVeg'. He was a Swede, after all. His arrival on the international scene coincided with the start of the 1970s, and Ronnie was the most dazzling member of an array of new stars set on establishing their reputations and eclipsing the likes of Stewart, Rindt, Hulme and Brabham.

To say that the people who worked with Ronnie adored him is no overstatement. As a journalist, one only has to pen a few words about the baby-faced blond Swede to prompt a handful of letters reflecting upon the good old days.

I first chatted to him, at Silverstone, on a bleak January day in 1970. The much-hyped March Engineering was putting on a press day to show off its new Type 701 Grand Prix cars. Chris Amon and Jo Siffert were there, as was Jackie Stewart, who was going to drive one of these new cars under the Tyrrell banner. Peterson was the quiet, tall Swede in the shaggy fur coat, who seemed to blend into the background as he waited for an opportunity to try the new machine.

He was very much March's baby. Plucked out of Formula 3, where he'd made his name racing a kart-like Italian Tecno, Ronnie had been signed on a three-year contract with March. In 1970, it was planned that he would drive an independent, semi-works 701, backed by enthusiast Colin Crabbe, after which he would vault into the works team for 1971 and 1972. In the minds of March co-founders Max Mosley, Robin Herd, Alan Rees and Graham Coaker, Ronnie Peterson was a key factor in the equation that would take their company to the summit of Formula 1.

Ronnie had car control. By this over-worked phrase, I'm not just talking about the ability to balance a car

Peterson made his Formula 1 debut with a March 701 entered by Colin Crabbe, pictured here during the British Grand Prix at Brands Hatch where he finished ninth.

on the outer limits of adhesion on a fast corner. Of course he could do that. But he was also an acrobat. He could wrap a car around his little finger, force it into performing contortions its designer had never imagined. Sure enough, these antics sometimes resulted in a shunt. Equally, they could yield memorable victories. He drove in 123 Grands Prix, winning ten of them, before dying from injuries sustained at Monza in 1978, when he was just 34-years-old. In retrospect, his life behind the wheel consists of a succession of snapshots, which gave us all a rare insight into a unique, outrageous talent.

As the March team was gradually assembled during the second half of 1969, so Alan Rees, in particular, became more convinced about Peterson's potential. Rees managed the highly successful Winkelmann Racing Formula 2 team throughout the 1960s, and for much of that time drove himself – as Jochen Rindt's running mate. Early in 1969, Max Mosley decided that he had had enough of trying to be a racing driver, and Winkelmann borrowed his Formula 2 Lotus 59B to enter Peterson in the important Albi race, in south-western France, as an exercise designed to give the Swede track experience. One man who felt that he absolutely had to be there was the engine preparation ace, Brian Hart, who immediately hopped into his Ford Escort and drove the nine-hour slog down to Albi to watch the young rising star for himself.

'During practice, Ronnie happened to go out of the pits in a rain shower and came up onto the tail of Jackie Stewart's Matra,' recalled Hart, 'and then kept up with him for five laps on a soaking track.

'You could see Stewart glancing in his mirrors, trying to work out who was chasing him. He could see that it was a Winkelmann Lotus, but it wasn't Graham or Jochen driving it. Stewart finally had to come into the pits to get rid of him. I think Alan and I were pretty sure after that, that Ronnie would one day win Grands Prix. It was obvious, just on the strength of those five laps.' So it proved, although Ronnie would have to wait until he moved to Lotus before breaking his Formula 1 duck.

Two seasons with the factory March team saw some excellent performances, although he struggled with the uncompetitive 721X – seen here at Monaco in 1972.

When Peterson joined Team Lotus in 1973 the prospect of victory was never far away – despite the frustrated expressions on the faces of team boss Colin Chapman and the Swede in this picture.

Four second places
in 1971 was good
enough for the
runner-up spot
in the World
Championship.

In 1971 he scored four second places in the March 711, and finished runner-up to Jackie Stewart in the World Championship. His star quality was also underlined by the manner in which he dominated the European Formula 2 Championship scene that season. But he also had more than his fair share of accidents. In the first Formula 2 race of the season, at Mallory Park, a steering-arm joint on his works March 712 seized, and he charged the bank, showering a group of spectators with debris from his car's shredded bodywork. But Ronnie walked away unhurt. More serious was his shunt during the Silverstone International Trophy meeting, where the throttles jammed opened. He slammed into the bank at Becketts, was briefly concussed, and came to in the ambulance on the way to Northampton hospital. Again, mercifully, he was unhurt.

In essence, these two episodes were a microcosm of Ronnie's racing life. He was forever teetering along that fine line which separates success from disaster. Yet, after that promising 1971 season in Formula 1, the Swede's fortunes waned uncomfortably for the next couple of years. March didn't come up with good enough equipment, and Ronnie was no development driver. He received tempting advances from Lotus boss Colin Chapman to join his team before his March contract was up, but Max Mosley – a qualified barrister – knew how to write a contract, and March was not letting its most prized human asset go before his current deal was up.

Finally, at the start of the 1973 season, Ronnie made the switch to Lotus. It was the convergence of great talents that we had all been waiting for. The Lotus 72 was at the peak of its technical development, and Peterson would surely fly from the moment he first climbed into its cockpit. Even for someone of Peterson's talent there would be a transitional period. Getting the best out of the 72 meant adopting a more

disciplined and restrained driving style. He needed to rein in his explosive technique before unleashing it in a more measured and controlled manner. It took three or four races before he'd got the best out of his new machine, by which time team-mate Emerson Fittipaldi had won three of the first four Grands Prix. He didn't win any more that season.

Ronnie won the French, Austrian, Italian and United States Grands Prix. In Austria, he had been content to play second fiddle to Emerson in the early stages, willing to help the Brazilian in his quest to retain the title. But when Fittipaldi stopped with a broken fuel line he went ahead to win. At Monza, Emerson ran in his wheel tracks for much of the way, and clearly expected to be waved ahead in the closing stages. But Chapman was issuing no such team orders – Fittipaldi's hopes of taking the title were almost gone anyway – and Ronnie was permitted to stay ahead. By this time, Emerson had decided he would switch to McLaren for 1974, which may have accounted for Chapman's reluctance to help his cause.

Ronnie was the favoured son and remained with Lotus, now joined by Jacky Ickx. He continued in fine form throughout the following year, and won another four races. But Chapman's planned replacement for the Type 72 – the over-complex and unreliable Lotus 76 – simply didn't work, so the old car had to race through to the end of 1975. It had been competing for six seasons.

At the start of 1976, Chapman made another major design blunder with the Lotus 77. This was more than enough for Ronnie. A deal was struck with his old employer, March Engineering, by means of which he left Lotus in exchange for the contract of another young Swedish star, Gunnar Nilsson. Many people felt that a simple, straightforward and uncomplicated car like the March 761 was all that Ronnie needed. The basic premise of this argument was sound

Then his career judgement went off the rails again. For 1977, he signed to drive for Ken Tyrrell's team, at the wheel of the radical P34 six-wheeler. It was a disastrous year. Ronnie couldn't come to terms with Ken's unyielding, disciplinarian line. The car was no good and, when it was running, Peterson usually found himself beaten by his team-mate, Patrick Depailler. His reputation seemed to have hit rock bottom. Yet he remained totally convinced he still had what it took to win races.

In 1978, he received an opportunity to prove that again when he rejoined Lotus, this time as team-mate to Mario Andretti. This was very much a number two arrangement, under which he had to support the American's title bid. Peterson rightly reasoned it was a small price to pay for the chance to restore his personal reputation. That chance to win again came sooner than he might have expected.

In the third race of the year, the South African Grand Prix, Ronnie found himself well wound up in a last lap chase of Depailler's Tyrrell, after Andretti had stopped for extra fuel in the closing stages. Down the daunting right-hander at Barbecue, Peterson was right on the Tyrrell's tail and, as they exited the flat-out Jukskei kink, the black and gold Lotus 78 was nailed to the Frenchman's gearbox. Ahead lay the tricky right-hander at Sunset, which led out onto a short straight before they would be hard on the brakes for the Clubhouse left-hander. Ronnie had only one shot left. Going into Sunset he took the outside line. Lotus and

enough, but Grand Prix racing was becoming more sophisticated in the mid-1970s, and the March was certainly not the last word in refinement. It was prone to excessive front tyre wear, for example. But, on the occasions that its handling was well balanced, Ronnie simply flew. He returned to the winner's circle at Monza with a well-judged victory in the Italian Grand Prix.

Laid-back Swede: with Lotus Team Manager, Peter Warr.

By the French Grand Prix of 1974 Peterson was a regular winner. This was his sixth triumph inside 20 races.

A brief spell back with March in 1976 did little for Peterson's career – although he did score a brilliant win at Monza. He then entered a period 'in the wilderness' with Tyrrell during 1977.

Tyrrell emerged from the corner side-by-side, banging wheels all the way to Clubhouse. Now the Lotus driver was on the inside line and accelerated cleanly away. Just two more corners, and Ronnie Peterson accelerated cleanly past the chequered flag to win by less than half a second. He had led only a single lap, but it was the one that mattered.

It was possibly the greatest win of Peterson's career – and the new Lotus 79 had yet to come on stream. That brilliantly successful machine would carry Andretti to that year's World Championship, and also furnish Ronnie with his second win of the season, in Austria. Yet it would be behind the wheel of the outdated Lotus 78 that the Swedish driver would sustain serious leg injuries, in a multiple pile-up, just after the start of the Italian Grand Prix.

He returned to Lotus in 1978 for a successful – and ultimately tragic – year as team-mate to Mario Andretti.

Over the following 12 hours reality seemed to have been suspended. The initial prognosis was good. Sure enough, Ronnie had suffered serious injuries, but he would make a full recovery and race again. By breakfast time on Monday morning he was dead, killed by a bone marrow embolism which had entered his bloodstream. The sense of loss lingers to this day. I can take you to the very point in the Monza paddock where I spoke to him for the last time on the morning of that race. Even now, the entire episode feels surreal and beyond belief.

James Hunt

I FIRST MET JAMES HUNT in the summer of 1968. I was 21 years old, four months his senior. We were at Snetterton, that bleak Norfolk airfield circuit, where he was driving a dark blue Russell Alexis Formula Ford car. I was a club reporter for *Autosport* magazine; a part-time journalist who earned a crust working in a London bank from Mondays to Fridays.

Several things struck me about James. He had an unusually firm handshake, and he was confident to the verge of aggressiveness. He seemed to have a very clear idea of where he was going and, clearly, concentrated on keeping himself extremely fit. For the next 25 years our careers ran in parallel, his through Formula 3 and into Formula 1, to the World Championship and then, an active retirement. I was fortunate enough to report on all his Grands Prix, from Monaco in 1973 – when he made his debut in the Hesketh team's March 731 – right through to that same race six years later, when he retired his Wolf WR7 and suddenly announced he would race no more.

The high spot of his career came at Japan's Mount Fuji circuit in the autumn of 1976. Having clawed his way to within hailing distance of the World Championship crown, James was presented with a golden opportunity when his key rival, Niki Lauda, withdrew after barely a lap; the Austrian convinced that the monsoon conditions were absurdly dangerous. That left Hunt's McLaren storming away from the field in a ball of spray. Victory in this crucial final race of the season was surely in the bag. Then came a punctured left front tyre that saw the Englishman's car scraping into the pits on its belly. The tyre was replaced, James resumed and drove the race of his life. He had no idea where he was at the finish, but he was sufficiently angered by his unscheduled pit stop to erupt from the car and roundly berate the McLaren Team Manager, Teddy Mayer, for what he thought was a last minute loss of the title. It took a couple of moments before he was calmed down sufficiently to realise that Mayer was holding up three fingers. 'Third,' he said. 'You're third, James. You are World Champion.'

Today, many Formula 1 stars would be clattering away from the race in a helicopter as soon as the television interviews had been dealt with. But on that memorable evening James stayed in the paddock and drank heartily with the rest of us right through until midnight. And oh, how we drank! The celebrations had enabled him to unwind; to relax from that state of acute nervousness that always seemed to be a necessary prerequisite if he was to drive at the peak of his form. He always seemed to be tottering on the brink of control; his nervous laughter and apparent zest for life acting as a kind of safety valve. Hindsight is a wonderful asset, but it was only some time after James's death that the world learnt of his susceptibility to black, overwhelming depressions. Looking back, it seems possible to discern those signs.

The transformation of this son of a London stockbroker from the ranks of precarious Formula 2 also-ran to front-running Grand Prix ace took little more than four years. Yet while the public school-educated Englishman was made of 'the right stuff', it was not always so obvious that he had the necessary star quality to go all the way. But there was something about him that suggested that, if got his hands on the right machinery, he would reach the summit of his profession. His progress in Formula 3 was spectacular, erratic and very fast, but he was frequently saddled by uncompetitive cars. It was only thanks to the ebullient Lord Hesketh that he was able to obtain a year-old Formula 2 March in which to run a limited programme of races at the end of 1972.

That was the turning point. A group of us later journeyed out to São Paulo with him for a triple-race series of Formula 2 events. James duly demonstrated formidable resolve at the wheel but produced little in the way of results. He was always a big hit with the ladies and there were endless parties throughout the trip. For many of his extra-curricular escapades James teamed up with his old friend, Mike Hailwood, and the pair of them – sadly now both dead – gained a reputation as hell raisers of the first order. Many people concluded that all this socialising meant that he was not taking his racing seriously enough. The reality was very different.

For 1973, Hesketh decided to stop wasting time in Formula 2 and make the ambitious jump into Grand Prix racing with his own March. Hunt was well up to the task, finishing sixth at Monaco, fourth at

Silverstone and third at Zandvoort. But his best result was second, at Watkins Glen, where he finished a matter of yards behind Ronnie Peterson's Lotus 72. That performance told us everything we needed to know about his professionalism at this early stage in his career.

Hesketh commissioned its Chief Designer, Harvey Postlethwaite, to produce the team's own car – the type 308 – for the 1974 season, but although James would drive it to a memorable victory in the Silverstone International Trophy race, he would have to wait until 1975 before posting his first Grand Prix victory. That red letter day was at Zandvoort, where Hunt and the team produced a superbly-judged strategic performance in tricky wet and dry conditions, holding off Niki Lauda's Ferrari 312T in a straight fight all the way to the finish. It was a performance that said a lot for both drivers. It confirmed Hunt's absolute cool under pressure, and served as an endorsement of Lauda's shrewd thinking: six points for second place were better than risking a collision with the determined Hunt in a bid to take the lead.

After that, it was no great surprise that when Emerson Fittipaldi decided to abandon McLaren for the Copersucar team at the end of the year, James surfaced as the first choice for McLaren. He was recruited to drive alongside the German driver Jochen Mass, and immediately stamped his authority on the situation by taking pole for his first McLaren outing at the Brazilian Grand Prix. He then got into his winning stride with victory in the Spanish Grand Prix at Jarama – only for his car to be excluded for a dimensional infringement. McLaren appealed the decision and James's win was restored to the team.

But similar good fortune did not attend him at Brands Hatch, where he took the restart of the British Grand Prix (a first corner pile-up had effectively eliminated his race car) and won commandingly from Niki Lauda's Ferrari on the road. That race represented the most controversial single episode in James's career. He was initially permitted to take the restart because it was believed that his car was still running when the race was red-flagged. Several witnesses testified that this was not so, and that Hunt had actually parked up and was out of the car before the red flag was shown. Some accused him of being disingenuous. Either way, he was ultimately disqualified from the race and the win handed to Niki Lauda, whose Ferrari had finished second on the road.

There were inevitably tensions between Niki and James, but the friendship between them ran sufficiently deep that it was not to be derailed by short-term problems. Outwardly, they had very different personalities, but their sense of mutual respect and affection was genuine, far removed from the cosmetic and insincere 'chumming up' which would be dished out for public consumption a couple of decades later between drivers who, in truth, hated the sight of each other.

Hunt's title hopes received a mathematical boost when Niki was badly burned at the Nürburgring, but within six weeks the Austrian had forced himself back into the cockpit of his Ferrari to continue his title defence. The advantage then swung back in Niki's

Hunt established his Formula 1 credentials with a series of giant-killing performances at the wheel of the Hesketh.

Hunt joined McLaren in 1976, finishing the year as World Champion.

For a period of about 16 months between 1976–77, Hunt was probably the finest driver in Formula 1. Not bad for someone written off as 'Hunt the shunt'.

favour with the confirmation of Hunt's Brands Hatch disqualification. James was aghast, faced with the challenge of surmounting a 17-point deficit over the final three races if he was to win the title. For many observers, this was the defining moment in his professional career. Far from going to pieces, it gave him even greater focus. Storming, dominant victories in the Canadian and US Grands Prix brought him to within challenging distance of Lauda. Then came Suzuka and that dramatic reversal of fortune that led to the World Championship. He was now not only on top of the world, but also on top of his form.

For perhaps 16 months, from the summer of 1976 to the early autumn of 1977, James Hunt was probably the best driver in the world. His car control reflected his enormous confidence and he frequently went into races believing himself to be the man to beat. His demeanour was admirable, but it was gradually undermined as McLaren lost its competitive edge. The superb M23, in its fourth season by the time James won the title, had been supplanted by the new M26 early in 1977. The new machine was supposedly a stiffer, stronger and lighter version of what had gone before. But it was not enough. Lotus was busy re-writing the parameters of Grand Prix engineering with the sensational new Type 78 wing car. The M26 was off the pace.

As the 1977 season progressed, McLaren found themselves struggling to keep on the pace.

Fighting hard to stay in play, James found himself sucked into more than his fair share of controversy during 1977. Battling for the lead of the Dutch Grand Prix, at Zandvoort, he was being pressed hard by Mario Andretti's Lotus 78. The American tried to run round the outside of Hunt on the 180-degree Tarzan right-hander at the end of the main straight. Rather than tightening his line, Hunt allowed the M26 to run wide and collided with the Lotus. After the race James remarked loftily: 'We don't overtake on the outside in Formula 1.' It was a crass observation. Andretti responded: 'I've got news for him. Where I come from we overtake any place we can.'

Later in the season, during the Canadian Grand Prix at Mosport Park, James was again forced to drive the McLaren on its door handles in order to keep ahead of Andretti. Coming up to lap his team-mate, Jochen Mass, James was momentarily balked, allowing Andretti through into the lead. James then crashed heavily, and punched a marshal who had come to his aid. His self-discipline seemed to be slipping.

The downward spiral continued in 1978, by which time James began to make silly mistakes. His concentration seemed to be wavering and his realisation that Grand Prix cars were things that could bite you had come, apparently as a complete shock, rather late in the day. By the end of 1978 it was clear that the

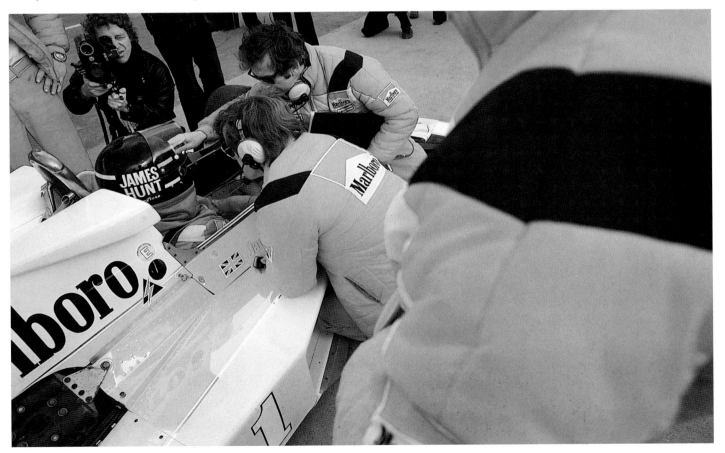

McLaren-Hunt alliance had run out of steam. Both had had sufficient of the other. James sought rejuvenation with the Wolf team from the start of 1979. But Wolf was another team whose star was waning, and there was to be no Indian Summer for either party.

Not yet quite 32, Hunt decided to quit racing after the Monaco Grand Prix. It seemed the right thing to do at the time and he freely confessed that he never really regretted his decision. It has to be said that even some of his closest friends found Hunt a pain in the butt at the height of his Formula 1 career, but that rather tiresome streak evaporated quickly in retirement as mellow middle age approached. He teamed up with Murray Walker to form a brilliant double act on the BBC television commentary team, and his perceptive observations behind the microphone were given added weight by the fact that he had first-hand experience of the sport.

The news of his sudden death from a heart attack, in June 1993, broke like a thunderclap to leave the motor racing world stunned beyond belief. He was a fine racing driver, truly endowed with a burning competitive spirit, but he was an even finer man. He was a naturally convivial personality who could, latterly at least, demonstrate considerable generosity of spirit and bestow unstinting praise upon others.

Above and left
A disappointing final season with Wolf brought Hunt's racing career to a close after the Monaco Grand Prix.

Overleaf
Watkins Glen 1976, where victory brought the World Championship within the Englishman's grasp.

Carlos Reutemann

THERE IS A HANDFUL OF GRAND PRIX DRIVERS who really deserved to win the World Championship yet failed to do so. Stirling Moss may be the most obvious example, but few would disagree that Carlos Alberto Reutemann is another. The brooding Argentine ace enjoyed a Formula 1 career spanning 11 seasons, until his sudden retirement after just two races of the 1982 season had been completed. On his day, he was pretty well unbeatable.

Yet, by the same token, Reutemann had moments when he seemed to be taking his time. If he could sniff the prospect of victory, then few drivers were more motivated or relentless. But on his off-days he could be positively indifferent. It was almost as if the motivation evaporated from his very soul. In those circumstances you could see gloom and depression written all over his face.

Reutemann first came to Europe in 1970, as a member of the Formula 2 Brabham team sponsored by the country's national automobile club. His team-mate was the former motorcyclist Benedicto Caldarella, who proved generally uncompetitive and was later replaced by Carlos Ruesch. Reutemann was quick from the start – although there was initially an over-zealous quality to his driving which got him into a few scrapes.

His nickname 'Lole' was a legacy of his childhood years. In Spanish, pigs are *Los Lechones* with a silent 's' in the 'Los'. When asked at school what he father did, he replied that he had a pig farm. It sounded like 'Lolechones', which was eventually reduced to 'Lole'. The tag stays with him to this day.

In 1971, Reutemann emerged as a top contender for the prestigious European Formula 2 Trophy series. Throughout the season he gathered competitive momentum, to the point where he was challenging the pre-season favourite, Ronnie Peterson, for Championship honours. Unfortunately for Reutemann his chances slipped away at the final round of the Championship, held at Rome's Vallelunga circuit. In scorching track conditions, the Argentine team opted to run Reutemann on harder grooved tyres, rather than the softer slicks that were fitted to Peterson's March. The Swede duly ran away with the race and the title.

Bernie Ecclestone had purchased the Brabham team in 1971, and Reutemann seemed a likely candidate for a drive the following year. He was obviously very talented and had access to some Argentine sponsorship. The two men met and the deal done.

Appropriately, Reutemann's World Championship debut came in front of his home crowd in Buenos Aires. He was driving the ex-Graham Hill Brabham BT34, which the veteran British driver had used to win the previous year's Silverstone International Trophy race. Carlos used it to great effect, getting the revitalised Brabham team off to an auspicious start by qualifying on pole position.

Come the race the Brabham lads got carried away with their own sense of achievement. Mistakenly opting to run the same soft Goodyear compound they had used for qualifying, Reutemann was off the pace from the start. He eventually finished seventh.

Carlos was indeed a challenger, but never a Formula 1 Champion.

Opposite page
Reutemann's five seasons with Brabham, culminating with a troubled 1976 in the BT45, yielded four Grand Prix victories.

Above and opposite top
**Two years with Ferrari –
1977–78 – brought five
more wins, but still the
Championship eluded
Reutemann.**

A few weeks later he won the non-Championship race held at São Paulo's Interlagos circuit, as a trailer for the following year's Brazilian Grand Prix. What followed was a patchy season for Reutemann, punctuated by a broken ankle sustained when he crashed a Formula 2 Brabham at Thruxton. He quickly recovered, but there was little in terms of hard results on the Formula 1 scene until he bagged fourth place in the Canadian Grand Prix at Mosport Park.

That Reutemann possessed a ruthless streak, thinly-disguised, was obvious. For much of the Canadian race his Brabham BT37 ran ahead of Denny Hulme's McLaren M19A, and although the Kiwi eventually found a way past he was speechless with rage about what he saw as the Argentine driver's unacceptably obstructive driving. In those days, 'protecting your line' was regarded as something which was not quite the ticket, and several drivers became rather wary of Reutemann from that moment on.

**The switch from Ferrari
to Lotus for 1979 failed
to reap dividends.**

Opposite bottom
**Formula 1's engima:
if the Argentine driver's
mood was right, then
no-one could touch him
for sheer speed in a
Grand Prix car.**

In 1973, the works Brabham team went into action with the distinctive pyramid-monocoque BT42, the first complete Formula 1 design to spring from Gordon Murray's drawing board. Both Carlos and his new` team-mate, Wilson Fittipaldi, were highly impressed with the new car. At the Spanish Grand Prix, at Montjuich Park, Reutemann simply flew. He might well have posted a debut victory for the car had he not been sidelined with a driveshaft joint failure in the closing stages of the race.

He finished only seventh in the 1973 Drivers' World Championship, but the following year he emerged as a serious contender for overall honours. Gordon Murray processed his Formula 1 design philosophy a crucial step further and came up with the superb Brabham BT44. By the third lap of the Argentine Grand Prix, at Buenos Aires, 'Lole' was through into the lead in front of his adoring home crowd.

But there was to be a cruel sting in the tail. With just one and a half miles left to the chequered flag, the

Armed with the 1981 Williams FW07B, Reutemann was in contention for the World Championship – only for it to slip from his grasp in the final race.

Brabham ground to a standstill – its tanks almost bone-dry. Immediately prior to the start of the race, the mechanics had been in something of a rush to change a faulty wheel bearing. In the panic it seems that a five-gallon churn had not been tipped into the tank. It was the only conceivable explanation.

Reutemann was desolate. A fortnight later he failed to mount a competitive challenge at Interlagos, but in round three – the South African Grand Prix at Kyalami – he finally broke his Formula 1 duck. Later that year he would win again, at the Österreichring, and again at Watkins Glen, where he headed team-mate Carlos Pace across the line in a Brabham 1–2 which certainly put a smile on Bernie Ecclestone's face.

Brabham insiders began to wonder whether Reutemann was angry about Pace's inclusion in the team, mid-season. Up until that point 'Lole' had been top dog alongside a succession of less talented team-mates. Now there was a man of unquestioning ability in the second car and, to add insult to injury, he was another South American!

In 1975 Carlos managed only a single victory, at the Nürburgring. From the touchlines, one could detect that the fire was going out of the Ecclestone–Reutemann partnership. It was – at first – an almost imperceptible process, but the pressure for change gathered steadily throughout the season. Ecclestone certainly rated Reutemann among the very best, but his increasingly perfunctory attitude

towards racing drivers in general meant that the Brabham boss had less time to accomodate the subtleties of his lead driver's character and moods. As a result, Carlos began to feel unsettled within the Brabham environment.

His mood was scarcely enhanced when Bernie signed to use Alfa Romeo flat-12 engines at the start of 1976. After years of signing the cheques for Cosworth-DFV rebuilds, Ecclestone had at last decided that a partnership with a works engine supplier was the only way to go. Unfortunately, the first Alfa engines were horrendous. The new BT45 debuted well over the weight limit and there it stayed for much of the season – thanks to its prodigious appetite for fuel. The 1976 season unfolded into an enduring nightmare. Pace managed to sustain his zestful enthusiasm, but Reutemann stopped even bothering to pretend. After the Dutch Grand Prix he bought himself out of the Brabham contract – an expensive move – and lined himself up with a Ferrari seat for 1977.

Intially, Reutemann's timing seemed suspect. Niki Lauda was just beginning his fightback after abandoning the 1976 Japanese Grand Prix, and was absolutely determined to restore his mastery over the Italian team. Carlos won superbly at Interlagos, but thereafter Niki ensured the advantage went in his direction. By the end of the season Lauda had clinched his second title after scoring three race wins. Reutemann failed to score again that year.

He turned that all around in 1978. Armed with Michelin's new radial rubber he stormed to four wins, carrying him to third place in the Championship. Despite this, the Ferrari squad never quite warmed to the slightly dour Argentine driver in the way that they would embrace his team-mate, Gilles Villeneuve, nor, indeed, Carlos's successor, Jody Scheckter. And all this despite the fact that Reutemann was at the absolute peak of his career and driving brilliantly.

He was tantalised – perhaps understandably – by the Lotus 79s which had outrun him to first and second places in the title battle, and readily accepted Colin Chapman's invitation to join the team for 1979. But by then the type 79 was yesterday's news, and sixth place in the Championship was all he could muster. By the end of the year, Reutemann was in negotiations with the Williams team, whose new FW07 ground-effect challenger had picked up Lotus's fallen baton. He signed as number two to Alan Jones and took a little time to get into the swing of things. He won at Monaco, but that was it.

Williams had a Ferrari-style agreement with Jones and Reutemann: if the team's cars were running first and second, and had an armlock on the race, then Alan was to win. At a rain-soaked Rio in 1981 this proved too much for the Argentinian, who could not bring himself to relinquish a commanding win. He stayed ahead to the finish.

After the race came the recriminations. Behind closed garage doors Jones lost his temper in a big way. Williams responded by failing to pay Reutemann his winner's cheque from the race. Carlos was shrewd enough never to mention the matter, an indication of just what an intelligent man he was.

Did he mind signing as number two to Jones? 'No,' he admitted, 'because I was in the middle of the shit with Lotus. When you are a starving man, you eat rabbit food if necessary. You are thankful for anything you can get.' Reutemann employed a cerebral approach to his motor racing which was very like that subsequently displayed by the great Ayrton Senna. If you watched him in the pit lane there were times when he seemed to be stalking his car, his dark eyes trying to bore through its surface in an attempt to gain some inner understanding of how it might perform. But Carlos needed tender loving care, and Williams was not equipped to provide emotional life support systems for its drivers.

With wins in the Brazilian and Belgian Grands Prix, Reutemann picked up the pace of his Championship challenge through 1981, assisted by the fact that Jones – the 1980 Champion – encountered more than his fair share of misfortune. Yet after the British Grand Prix at Silverstone, where he finished second to John Watson's McLaren, Reutemann made a bet with me that he would not

win the World Championship. He was 17 points ahead at the time. I suspect a psychiatrist would have had a field day with that one.

At the final race of the season, the Las Vegas Grand Prix at Caesar's Palace, he was poised to take the title. He qualified on pole, stunning the opposition into silent submission. But on race morning he touched another car with his left front suspension and the wishbone had to be replaced before the start. 'The car never handled properly again,' explained Reutemann. The Williams crew watched in disbelief as he faded to seventh in the race. Nelson Piquet won the title by a single point.

At the start of 1982, Reutemann opened his campaign with a strong second place in the South African Grand Prix, before retiring in Brazil. Then, with his 40th birthday just weeks away, he told Frank Williams that he was retiring – there and then.

Did he feel that his new team-mate, Keke Rosberg, was going to offer too much competition? Or did he have prior knowledge that Argentina was likely to invade the Falklands a few months later? That would have certainly made his position at Williams virtually untenable. It made you think.

Reutemann, pictured here in the 1980 Williams FW07, failed to match the competitive zeal shown by his Australian team-mate, Alan Jones.

Jody Scheckter

FEW DRIVERS HAVE STARTED their international racing careers with such a wild reputation, yet retired from the cockpit so highly regarded as an astute and tactical operator. South African Jody Scheckter was just 22 years old when he made his Grand Prix debut in 1972, and he retired at the youthful age of 30. During the intervening years he contested 112 Grands Prix, winning nine of them together with the 1979 World Championship for Ferrari.

In his early days, Jody was always a headline maker. He arrived in Britain at the start of 1971 having won a prize as South Africa's most promising young driver. Part of the award was a Formula Ford Merlyn, with which he dominated the British national series, before storming through Formula 3 and then European Formula 2 at the wheel of a semi-works McLaren. He entered the history books as the winner of the last Formula 2 international to be held at London's Crystal Palace circuit, and then McLaren entered him in a third M19A for the US Grand Prix at Watkins Glen. He looked as though he had been born in the cockpit, qualifying as high as eighth on the grid and only losing the chance of a possible top six finish after a spin.

His maiden Grand Prix drive had come about as a direct result of tension that had built up between Jody and the McLaren team during the summer of 1972. He had been approached to drive a privately-owned, Lucky Strike-backed Lotus 72 entered by his compatriot, Dave Charlton. But his contract with McLaren required him to give at least three weeks notice in the event of a deal like this coming up. So Jody had to let it pass. Shortly afterwards, however, Colin Chapman offered him a drive in the Lotus 72 for the last four races of the season – in place of Dave Walker. He advised the McLaren management of this offer, and they promply hit the roof.

'They explained, quite forcefully, the extent of their investment in me,' recalled Scheckter. 'And made the point that I had as much a moral as a legal obligation not to go somewhere else during the period of my agreement with them. For my part, I felt that they had an equal obligation to provide me with at least the occasional Formula 1 drive, once I had proved that I could hold my own in Formula 2.' After a quiet discussion with Denny Hulme, who told him that the number two Lotus seat was traditionally a passport to nowhere, Jody sent a 'Thanks, but no thanks' message back to Chapman.

One of the highlights of Scheckter's career was victory for the brand new Wolf team in Argentina, 1977 – the car's first outing.

Two years at Ferrari
yielded the World
Championship title
and three wins.

But his retirement at the
end of 1980 went almost
unnoticed after a bitterly
disappointing season.

Three years with Tyrrell yielded four wins including one – in Sweden, 1976 – with the unique P34 six-wheeler.

In truth, Jody was the most exciting young talent on the international horizon. Not only was he fearless and dynamically quick, he also had a confidence bordering on aggression which the McLaren squad – at that time a touch elitist and defensive – tended to fuel. They knew their new young kid was something special and were not about to underplay his status. For 1973, he competed in the US Formula 5000 series – winning the Championship – and had some Can-Am outings as well. Nothing seemed too demanding or powerful for the young South African, and he cultivated this wild boy image by turning up at US press conferences barefoot. He was quite an operator.

On the Formula 1 front he was given a second guest drive on his home turf at Kyalami, where he qualified his McLaren M19C on the front row of the grid. He failed to finish, but the race was won by his team-mate Denny Hulme. The craggy New Zealander got on well with the young Scheckter, taking him under his wing to some extent. Hulme, nicknamed 'The Bear,' was notoriously wary and uncommunicative when it came to dealing with journalists, and he suffused Jody with the same nervous caution. It was no surprise, therefore, that Jody found himself with a new sobriquet – 'Baby Bear' – by the middle of the 1973 season. But the most appropriate nickname of all was surely 'Fletcher', after the baby seagull in the novel *Jonathan Livingstone Seagull*, which tried to fly when it was too young and kept crashing into the cliff face.

The 1973 French Grand Prix saw Jody installed in one of the splendid new McLaren M23s, and starting again from the front row at the Circuit Paul Ricard. He went straight into the lead and so frustrated the chasing Emerson Fittipaldi that the Brazilian dived inside him on a tight corner and the two cars collided. Emerson, the reigning World Champion, was furious about Jody's driving, but the McLaren lad shrugged it all aside.

A couple of weeks later he was involved in another multiple shunt, this time at the end of the opening lap of the British Grand Prix at Silverstone. Coming into Woodcote – then a flat-out, eye-of-a-needle right hander unsullied by chicanes – Scheckter ran wide onto the grass and spun back into the pit wall. Cars dodged left and right as they tried to avoid the stricken McLaren, but the net result was a pile-up involving more than a dozen cars. The race was flagged to a halt. It was later restarted, without Jody and many of his competitors, and was won by McLaren's Peter Revson. Thereafter Scheckter would only drive two more races – the Canadian and US Grands Prix – before he was signed to Tyrrell for 1974, as successor to Jackie Stewart. It seemed that the McLaren management, perhaps quite understandably on the basis of its own experiences to date, judged that Jody might be too expensive in terms of damaged equipment. This was no more perspicacious a decision than the one they would take four years later, when they decided against retaining Gilles Villeneuve for ostensibly similar reasons.

Driving for Tyrrell from the start of 1974 meant picking up the baton left by Jackie Stewart after his retirement. The original plan had been for Jody to partner François Cevert, but the Frenchman's death during practice at Watkins Glen the previous year had broken that thread of continuity. Scheckter instead found himself paired with Patrick Depailler. It was very much a novice partnership.

He found the short-chassis Tyrrell 006 – the 1973 Championship-winning car inherited from Stewart – very difficult to drive. Later in the season, the longer wheelbase 007 arrived and Scheckter won both the Swedish and British Grands Prix. Going into the final race at Watkins Glen, he was in contention for the Championship. Admittedly, his was an outside bet. To take the title in his first full year of Formula 1 racing, Jody had to win the race with Emerson Fittipaldi (McLaren) and Clay Regazzoni (Ferrari) outside the top five. But a fuel line broke and he was immediately out of the equation, leaving Emerson to finish fourth and take his second crown.

In 1975, Jody opened the season with an emotional victory in his home race, the South African Grand Prix. But that would prove to be his only win of the season. Having finished third in the previous year's Championship, he now slumped to seventh in the final order. Tyrrell then proceeded to stun the motor racing world with the introduction of its radical P34 six-wheeler. It carried Scheckter and Depailler to a 1–2 finish in the 1976 Swedish Grand Prix at Anderstorp, repeating their 1974 success, but that was as far as it went. By the end of the season it was clear that the Tyrrell–Scheckter alliance was running out of steam. The magical gloss had worn off their partnership, and Jody looked elsewhere for 1977.

What followed proved an inspired decision. In 1976, the Austro-Canadian oil millionaire, Walter Wolf, had purchased Frank Williams's ailing Grand Prix team and eventually decided that he would effectively start from scratch. He recruited the former Hesketh designer, Harvey Postlethwaite, to build an all-new car; the former Lotus manager, Peter Warr, to run the team, and Scheckter to drive it. On the face of it this was a big risk. But, on closer examination, the venture was not quite as speculative as it might have looked. All the elements were in place for a successful partnership and, remarkably, they gelled quickly enough for Jody to win the first race of the season, the Argentine Grand Prix at Buenos Aires.

The Wolf WR1 was an agile, serviceable and uncomplicated design, powered by the ubiquitous Cosworth DFV engine. The theory was to give Jody a straightforward car and let him do the rest. He added

The 1978-vintage 'ground-effect' Wolf WR6 *(left)* failed to match the success of its predecessor.

the Monaco and Canadian Grands Prix to his victory tally that season, and finished second in the World Championship behind Ferrari's Niki Lauda.

But in 1978 he slumped back to seventh overall. The new ground-effect WR6 was impressive, but not quite good enough to add to Scheckter's tally of Grand Prix victories. At the end of the year, he took what seemed to be the biggest gamble of his career. He signed to drive for Ferrari.

Jody now had the experience to compliment his racer's edge. His priority was to win the World Championship and he judged that Ferrari offered him the most positive environment within which he was likely to achieve that aim. In signing for Maranello, he was sufficiently shrewd to appreciate that all might not be straightforward. Nor might it be an easy task to beat sitting tenant Gilles Villeneuve in a straight fight. That latter point was thrown into sharp focus early in the year, when Gilles beat him into second place in both the South African and Long Beach Grands Prix. Kyalami was a tactical wet-dry race where the cards simply fell against him, but around the streets of Long Beach Villeneuve simply beat him fair and square.

None of this ruffled Jody, and the manner in which he kept his nerve throughout the season – and never ventured a word of criticism to the team – was extremely impressive. His even-tempered approach would net him the World Championship crown.

JODY SCHECKTER

'I made the decision to join Ferrari, and that was that,' he explained later. 'It may sound funny, but I didn't care whether a car was good or bad once I'd signed a contract. If it was bad, then I just had to consider that I'd been unlucky and made a bad decision. You have to do the best you can. The only time to worry is when you are negotiating contracts at the start of a season.

'As far as Gilles was concerned,' he continued, 'I would probably have won the Championship earlier in the season if I hadn't had such a fast team-mate. But he made some mistakes, mistakes that probably cost him a chance of the title. It all worked out for me. I did not get flustered under pressure and try too hard which, on the face of it, I might have done with Gilles going so quickly.

'He was a good driver, very good. But I saw things in his driving that I used to do when I was younger. He regularly dropped wheels onto the dirt, whereas I tried to keep the car off the kerb. Sure, he kept up the pressure, but I always felt confident.'

Jody won the Belgian, Monaco and Italian Grands Prix to clinch his title crown. And Gilles' sense of honour meant that he was not challenged as he led from the start of the decisive race at Monza. Ferrari team orders dictated that whichever driver was ahead

when the team's cars took first and second places should remain ahead. As a result, Gilles followed in Jody's wheel tracks all the way to the finish, despite knowing that if he overtook the South African then he would win the Championship for himself. That he never so much as considered doing so says as much about Villeneuve's sense of honour as it does about the relationship between the two men.

The Ferrari 312T4 had carried the team's two drivers to a total of six victories thanks to its mechanical reliability and the consistency of its Michelin tyres. Aerodynamically, however, it was painfully lacking, and when Williams and Ligier raised the stakes in 1980, so the revised Ferrari T5 suddenly slipped down the field

into the role of also-ran. World Champion in 1979, Jody scored just two points the following season to end up 19th in the final title stakes. Long before that final tally was fixed in stone, he announced that he would be retiring at the end of the season. With dignity and precious little in the way of fanfares, he slipped off the Grand Prix stage for good.

By the end of his career, Jody had developed an appealing, self-deprecatory humour. He has retained his gentle manner, living quietly in retirement in London after more than a decade building up a prosperous and successful business in the United States. In the ten years following his retirement, he watched just two Grands Prix.

Scheckter's championship signalled the start of a period in the wilderness for Ferrari.

John Watson

IT IS POPULARLY BELIEVED THAT JOHN WATSON lacked the hard edge of ambition to capitalise on his spectacular natural talent behind the wheel of a Grand Prix car. This may be an over-harsh judgement. Certainly there is plenty of evidence to support the Ulsterman's claim that he was as hard as anybody was in terms of wheel-to-wheel determination. Perhaps it was out of the car where he really lacked the stealth and negotiating ruthlessness which so characterised, for example, Niki Lauda, his Brabham-Alfa team-mate throughout 1978.

Watson contested 152 Grands Prix between 1973-85. He won five of them and came within sight of the 1982 World Championship. His chief rival, Keke Rosberg, eventually pipped him to the post in the final race of the season and – in fairness – went into the last round as favourite. Yet the fact remains that 'Wattie' came close to achieving his life's ambition on a scorching afternoon in Las Vegas.

One could argue that John arrived on the scene a decade or so too late. Not in terms of his own age, but in terms of the era in which he raced. He had a classical touch to his driving. He was a naturally gifted performer, but he did not always get the best out of his machinery. As Grand Prix cars became more complex to set up during the late 1970s and early 1980s, so Watson sometimes found himself at a distinct performance disadvantage.

Austria 1976: 'Wattie' takes his maiden Grand Prix win with the promising Penske.

A mild-mannered, pleasant man, he grew up in a motor racing environment. His father Marshall, a prosperous Belfast motor trader, had won the first saloon car race to be held in Ireland – at the wheel of a Citroen Light 15 – in the early 1950s. He encouraged his only son's racing ambitions and backed them with the necessary cash in the days when international Formula 2 was just about manageable for a privateer. At the wheel of an outdated Lotus 48, John laid down a marker for the future with a heady drive through the field in the 1969 Easter Monday Formula 2 race at Thruxton. In those days, the top Formula 2 international events were watched by motor racing insiders with as much fascination as any Grand Prix. Leading Formula 1 stars competed in comparable cars against ambitious newcomers. This particular race may have ended against an earth bank, but John's performance turned a few heads.

In 1970, Marshall bought his son a brand new Brabham. Unfortunately, tyre failure caused him to crash heavily at Rouen and he had to sit out much of the season. In 1971, he resumed racing in Formula 2 and enjoyed a moderately good season. The next two years saw him getting by as what might be described as a 'jobbing actor' on the international racing stage. Picking up drives here and there in Formula 2 and sports cars, he earned a crust and forged a decent reputation. If somebody could only give him a chance, then surely he would prove he could make the grade.

Watson was competitive in the 1977-vintage Brabham-Alfa Romeo, but failed to match outright speed with points finishes and, of course, victories.

For 1978 he found himself rather overshadowed by his team-mate, Niki Lauda, who was the reigning World Champion.

Watson's greatest successes came with the new-look McLaren team.

used by the works pairing of Carlos Reutemann and Carlos Pace. A fine fourth place in Austria, despite wrestling with a blistered tyre, duly followed.

Through no fault of his own, Watson was the beneficiary of other people's misfortunes at two key moments during his career. Having signed to drive for Surtees in 1975, he was given the opportunity to switch to the Penske team, following the untimely death of Mark Dononhue during the Austrian Grand Prix weeked. And again, three years later, he was recruited to drive for McLaren at the start of 1979, after his old friend Ronnie Peterson was killed at Monza. In between those two unexpected and tragic turning points, however, Watson had matured into a first-rate driver in his own right.

It was with Penske that Watson finally became his own man. Previously, there was always a suspicion among those who didn't know him well that he was little more than a good second stringer who had occasional flashes of brilliance. Yet at Penske he proved he was better than that. His great day came in the 1976 Austrian Grand Prix at the Österreichring. Running at the front throughout Watson, in the Penske PC3, saw off a firm challenge from James Hunt's McLaren to post the team's maiden Formula 1 victory. It looked as though this might be the first of many, particularly when Watson reproduced this form at Zandvoort, and hounded Hunt for lap after lap until the Penske's gearbox wilted under the strain. But Penske was not totally committed to Formula 1. At the end of the season its prime sponsor decided to withdraw, and the American operation withdrew from the Grand Prix scene in order to concentrate on the Indycar series.

Watson's consequent spell of unemployment proved happily brief. Bernie Ecclestone snapped him up to partner Carlos Pace in the Brabham-Alfa squad, and John rewarded his new team chief's faith in him by snatching second place on the grid for the first race of the season, the Argentine Grand Prix at Buenos Aires. He also led the race briefly, but retired when the rear suspension tried to break away from its anchors on the gearbox casing. Formula 1 could be quite a lurid business, even in the 1970s.

Both Watson and Pace failed to finish at Interlagos, and both were off the pace again in South Africa, but the team was rocked by a major body blow only a few weeks later. Just after Watson qualified his Brabham on pole for the Brands Hatch Race of Champions, news came through from Brazil that Pace had been killed in a light aircraft crash near São Paulo. The tragedy propelled Watson into the *de facto* team leadership. To some extent Pace had grown into the role of the team's golden boy, having persevered doggedly with the troublesome Brabham-Alfa throughout 1976 when Reutemann's interest had

In the spring of 1973, he was invited by Bernie Ecclestone to drive the new Brabham BT43 in the Brands Hatch Race of Champions. Unfortunately, the throttle stuck open and he suffered another heavy accident, fracturing one leg. But Ecclestone had seen enough of Watson to be impressed. Later that summer he got his Championship break when he was invited to drive a Brabham BT37 in the British Grand Prix. He was on his way.

At the beginning of the following year he signed to drive a private Brabham for the London car dealer, Paul Michaels, who owned the successful 'Hexagon of Highgate' business. The distinctive chocolate liveried Brabham BT43 carried him to his first Championship point, with a sixth place finish at Monaco. Later in the season the team traded up to a BT44 – similar to that

faded. Now the hopes and aspirations of the team rested firmly on Watson's shoulders, with the young German driver, Hans-Joachim Stuck, recruited as his partner for the remainder of the year.

Anybody who had any doubts about Watson should consider his achievements in 1977. Pole position at Monaco; losing victory in France after fuel pick-up problems when there was less than a lap to go; dominating the early stages of the British Grand Prix. That lost victory at Dijon-Prenois was a particularly painful episode. Mario Andretti, the beneficiary of his misfortune, was sympathetic: 'Sure, I feel sorry for John,' he said. 'He did a beautiful job today and never made any mistakes that I saw.'

Watson finished a distant 13th in the 1977 Championship, a result that in no way mirrored his competitive position throughout the year. In 1978 everything changed with the arrival of Niki Lauda as his team-mate. On the face of it, the Austrian's arrival should not have changed Watson's status, but it had the effect of demoting him from number one to number two driver in everybody's eyes.

But, yet again, John emphasised that this was not necessarily true. He qualified second at Monaco with the BT46 and ran away from the pack in the early stages of the race, only to be slowed by brake problems that dropped him to an eventual fourth. By the end of the year he had finished sixth in the World Championship – highlighted by a fine third place in

the British Grand Prix – but was replaced by the Brazilian rising star, Nelson Piquet, for the following season.

'I had no problems at all with my relationship with either Niki or Bernie,' he recalled at the end of that season. 'It was fantastic working with Niki and we had more laughs and fun with each other than either of us had had with a team-mate before.

'Bernie was no problem, but I felt he did seem to like people with a more aggressive nature than I'd got. I'm not aggressive as such and I think he tends to measure racing drivers outside the car against Jochen Rindt. He was tough and ambitious, like Niki. I'm no less ambitious when I'm behind the wheel of a racing car, but there's no way I'm as aggressive in normal life.'

On leaving Brabham to join McLaren, John was so confident about his prospects for 1979 that he bet Bernie he would finish ahead of Niki in the Championship points table at the end of the year. He was absolutely on the button, although both fell well short of expectations. John finished ninth on 15 points with Niki 14th on four points, the Austrian having quit racing before the end of the season.

The McLaren team had pretty well lost its way by 1979, and its new ground-effect M28 proved an absolute disaster. John had started the year on an upbeat note, even talking in terms of a possible World Championship crown, but the reality could not have been bleaker. He and team-mate Patrick Tambay struggled abjectly and the team sanctioned the design of a brand new car, the M29, in time for the British Grand Prix. Watson drove it brilliantly through the field to finish fourth, as if to emphasise that his ability had not been dulled by consistent disappointment. But McLaren still had a long way to hobble before being merged with Ron Dennis's Project Four organisation in time for the 1981 season, when John would

win the British Grand Prix in the John Barnard-designed MP41.

For 1982 John found himself once again partnered alongside Niki Lauda, who had emerged from retirement to pick up the threads of his racing career. That year both drivers won two races apiece, even though their Cosworth-engined machines were beginning to look uncompetitive against the more powerful turbo opposition from Renault, Ferrari and BMW. Once again, Watson proved what a scintillating racer he could be by passing car after car through the tortuous streets of Detroit to add victory in this US race to his earlier success in Belgium. His final Grand Prix win came at Long Beach, in 1983, when he qualified 22nd and then, thanks to the higher ambient temperatures which prevailed on race day, took advantage of his Michelin rubber to carve through the field and win the race. In doing so he beat Lauda into second place, a result that gave him particular satisfaction.

At the end of that season he was unable to strike a deal to continue with McLaren. Alain Prost, who had driven alongside John in his freshman season in 1980, now came onto the market again after three years with Renault. Ron Dennis snapped him up and, apart from a single guest drive in the 1985 European Grand Prix at Brands Hatch, that was the end of John's Formula 1 career.

It's easy to say that he still had some mileage left in him when circumstances rode him out of front line racing. But his gentlemanly nature enabled him to conceal his disappointment, outwardly at least.

'I think McLaren and its sponsors were concerned,' he reflected, 'that they could be facing the prospect of both Lauda and myself retiring at the end of 1984, with the result that they would have to go out and buy somebody for top dollar. This way, they could get Prost at the bottom of the market.'

Alan Jones

ALAN JONES WAS PHYSICALLY TOUGH AND uncompromising; endowed with more than his fair share of self-belief. Perhaps he needed these qualities more than most, because he was not universally rated as a future World Champion as he scrambled up the Formula 3 ladder in the early 1970s. Yet while there may have been many more obviously talented drivers than this tough Australian, there were few who were more determined.

He had motor racing in his blood. His hard-living father, Stan, was one of his country's most successful racers of the immediate post-war era. A contemporary of Sir Jack Brabham, many rated Stan Jones as good – maybe even better – than the man who went on to win three World Championships. Yet Stan raced exclusively in Australasia, concentrating on his business interests rather than a professional racing career.

Alan certainly got his determination from his old man. In 1970 Stan Jones accompanied his son to Brazil, where he was driving a Formula 3 Brabham in the winter Torneio series. During the course of one of these races there was a dispute over an aspect of the Brabham's legality, which prompted the Lotus Team Manager to visit the Jones pit. Despite having suffered a succession of strokes, Stan Jones chased the unfortunate man away, brandishing his crutches.

Like his father, who made and then lost a fortune in the motor trade, Alan Jones lived on his wits during those financially precarious, hand-to-mouth years of the early 1970s. He teamed up with fellow Antipodeans Brian McGuire and Alan McCully to established the grandly-titled Australian International Racing Organisation – AIRO as it became known in British racing circles – to contest Formula 3 races, but they made the tactical error of buying the ex-works Formula 1 Brabham team transporter. This misleadingly created the impression that the Formula 3 organisation was extremely well-heeled and nobody showed any interest in sponsoring their activities. In fact this was far from the truth, and Alan devised a succession of schemes to support his racing aspirations – ranging from selling Volkswagen campers to various of his globe-trotting countrymen to opening a bed and breakfast establishment to cater for the same clientele.

By 1973, Alan had established himself as a leading runner on the British Formula 3 scene. But it was not obvious where he would go from there. By 1975 he had got a break at the wheel of a private Hesketh, then switched briefly to Graham Hill's team, before John Surtees offered him his big chance in 1976. At the wheel of the compact Surtees TS19 he scored seven points to finish 14th in the World Championship, which was a more promising result than it seemed to be on paper. Yet it was in the non-championship Race of Champions at Brands Hatch, in 1976, that Jones really displayed his mettle, leading half the distance in the TS19 before James Hunt's McLaren scrambled by to win with the Aussie chasing him across the line. Surtees could be a hard taskmaster, but the real reason that the TS19 never quite demonstrated its ultimate potential was lack of

France, 1980: Jones
took particular pleasure
in beating the Ligiers
in a straight fight on
home soil.

finance. Team Surtees had a relatively moderate budget by the standards of the time and never had money to spare for much in the way of research and development programmes.

Jones fell out with Surtees at the start of 1977, and it briefly looked as though his Formula 1 chance might have passed. But tragedy delivered an unexpected route back into the limelight. When Tom Pryce was killed during the South African Grand Prix, Jones was recruited to fill the vacant place in the Shadow team. Later that season, he manhandled the overweight and uncompetitive DN8 as high as second place in the Austrian Grand Prix. James Hunt's leading McLaren retired with engine trouble, and Alan was presented with his first Formula 1 win on a plate.

In 1978, Frank Williams was casting around for a

new driver to join his fledgling Grand Prix team. He eventually settled on Jones, paying him £40,000 pounds for his first season. At the wheel of the new Williams FW06, Jones was running in second place at Long Beach before fuel starvation intervened. At one point during the chase, Frank turned to a colleague on the pit wall and remarked, 'I really don't care if we don't finish this race, he's the most exciting driver I've seen since Ronnie Peterson.'

Alan grew with the team. He was a man's man and struck a chord with Williams, who was keen to challenge the establishment and stop being the butt of pit lane jokes after years of fielding a succession of second-rate cars. He wanted to make 'The Big Time' and he quickly reached the conclusion that Jones could take him there, given the right car. For 1979,

Williams designer Patrick Head produced just that, in the form of the new ground-effect Williams FW07.

Jones proved himself to be a brave and uncompromising driver. He was physically tough, even though he affected a dislike for physical exertion when it came to keeping fit. But he was blessed with a naturally-muscular body and great inherent stamina. One observer in 1981 observed that the sight of Jones, wearing his dark green overalls, put him in mind of a helicopter pilot on a mission in Vietnam.

Ironically, it was not Jones but his number two, Clay Regazzoni, who posted the Williams team's maiden Grand Prix victory, at Silverstone in 1979 – albeit after Alan had retired while well in the lead. But he only had to wait until the next race before getting in on the act, and thereafter that year scored four more victories.

Jones sustained this momentum right through the 1980 and 1981 seasons, and it was only a succession of trifling mechanical failures throughout 1981 that denied him back-to-back Championships. His 1980 title-clincher came at Montreal, where the race began with a multiple collision at the first corner and his

The new 'ground-effect' Williams FW07 was the perfect instrument for the tough Australian's charging style.

Five wins in 1980, including this one at Watkins Glen *(right)* secured the World Championship – the first for both Jones and the Williams team.

title rival, Nelson Piquet, was forced to take over the spare Brabham BT49. Unfortunately, this car was fitted with a highly-stressed qualifying engine, which failed to last the distance. Jones won quite easily.

Piquet would relieve him of his title in 1981, but it was a lucky break for the Brazilian – given the fact that Jones lost at least three certain wins from mechanical failure.

Ever the centre of controversy, Jones turned up at Monza in 1981 with a couple of broken fingers on one hand, the legacy of an altercation with a Transit van – and its occupants – on London's Chiswick High Road. Almost in passing, he remarked to Frank Williams that he had decided to retire at the end of the season. 'Thanks very ******* much!' replied Williams, who

now faced the prospect of losing his ace driver at a time when all other potential candidates were already signed up for 1982.

Jones would win the Italian Grand Prix, and repeat that success with a similarly impressive victory in the final race of the year at Las Vegas. Up until then, Williams still believed there might be a chance of persuading Jones to change his mind. After the season was over they flew him back to Britain to try the revolutionary six-wheeler Williams FW07D – with four tiny driven rear wheels – at Donington Park. Jones was impressed, but it was not enough to reverse his decision.

Jones lived in an era before the contrived breeze of political correctness began to blow through the Grand

Jones, typically, on the limit in the 1978 Williams FW06 at Kyalami, South Africa.

The Australian's title
defence in 1981 was
hampered by poor
reliability and bad luck.
Nevertheless he scored
two more wins – and
should have taken at
least three more.

Prix business. For example, he simply could not stand Carlos Reutemann – the man recruited to replace Regazzoni in the second Williams – and made no effort to conceal the fact. His animosity was aggravated still further after the Argentinian won in Brazil against team orders.

A couple of hours after Jones's final Grand Prix victory, Reutemann approached him and offered his wishes for a happy retirement. Under the circumstances, Carlos could have been forgiven for feeling gutted, as this was the race in which his own World Championship hopes had finally been wiped from the slate. Even so, he went through the motions:

'OK, Alan. Well, goodbye. Shall we bury the hatchet?' said Carlos. Jones looked at him and replied,

'Yeah, in your bleedin' back mate.' And that was it. He walked away.

Jones and Williams had been thrown together at a mutually advantageous moment. They gelled on a personal level and were both responsible, in part, for the launch of one another's careers. But while Williams continued onwards and upwards after the bluff Australian's departure, Alan's fortunes never quite blossomed again.

In 1983, he was briefly invited back to drive an Arrows A6 in the Long Beach Grand Prix. It was a commercial sprat to catch a mackerel, with the Arrows boss, Jack Oliver, hoping that the former World Champion's name would attract major sponsorship. The strategy did not work.

Two years later Jones was lured out of retirement to drive for the new Beatrice-Lola team, a grand and ambitious operation which had lavish funding and benefited from a works Ford engine deal. It was a big bucks offer which would help to top up Jones's depleted financial resources. But he was older now – nudging 40 – and his best days were certainly in the past. The project was not helped by the fact that the new Ford turbo engine was late being completed, and the team had to start racing with Brian Hart engines as an interim measure. This arrangement continued into the new season, and Jones did not get

his hands on the new Ford V6 until the San Marino Grand Prix at Imola. He showed some flair on occasion and bagged a handful of Championship points. But the exercise did nothing for his reputation; the team folded at the end of 1986 when its prime sponsor withdrew.

Most of his fans prefer to remember Alan Jones during his great days at Williams. They are days recalled with admiration by those who worked with a man who inspired great loyalty, and could single-handedly lift the morale of a team when things were not going well. A rare quality indeed.

The well-funded Beatrice-Lola outfit tempted Jones out of retirement, for the second time, in 1986. He was back home in Australia before the season was over.

113

Gilles Villeneuve

NOBODY COULD QUITE BELIEVE IT. The young Canadian driver in the McLaren M23 was tremendously quick but, goodness, did he spin a lot. The scene was Silverstone; the occasion, pre-qualifying for the 1977 British Grand Prix. There were 14 hopefuls going for the seven slots available to move up into qualifying proper, and Gilles Villeneuve was easily the quickest. He explained away his spins by saying that

he was in a hurry to learn the car, and that it made sense to drive over its limits deliberately in order to establish precisely where the limits were. On first acquaintance, this theory sounded like complete lunacy. But when one got to know the slight, beaming little French Canadian better it all made perfect sense.

There was never a Racer like Villeneuve. He had a delightfully simplistic philosophy, was not in the slightest bit worried about hurting himself and never gave anything less than 100% when he was behind the wheel of a racing car. His reflexes had been honed from an early age in the spectacular sport of snowmobile racing. Hurtling round half-mile ovals of packed snow and ice on 650cc-engined projectiles may not seem like everybody's idea of heaven, but this was where Gilles cut his competitive teeth from the age of eight years old.

Born in 1950 at Chambly, Quebec, Gilles would dominate this form of competition in Canada, yet it was not until 1973 that he would try his hand at motor racing with an elderly, locally-built Formula Ford car. Gradually, he struggled through the junior league before gaining a foothold in the North American Formula Atlantic series. In 1976, he won the prestigious Trois Rivières street race in Quebec, beating Formula 1 drivers Alan Jones and James Hunt in the process. With characteristic altruism, Hunt reported back to his McLaren boss, Teddy Mayer, that Villeneuve had enormous and obvious potential. Mayer duly offered him a contract to drive for five Grands Prix in 1977, although this eventually came down to nothing more than the British Grand Prix at Silverstone. Villeneuve qualified the M23 ninth fastest – two places ahead of Jochen Mass in the other works M26 – and might well have finished in the points had not a faulty water temperature gauge sent him into the pits, incorrectly believing the car was overheating. He eventually finished tenth.

Villeneuve was unquestionably a huge talent, and McLaren retained an option on his services for 1978. But a few weeks later Mayer announced that he was not taking up that option, instead preferring to sign Frenchman Patrck Tambay.

'Gilles looked as though he might be a bit expensive on the machinery,' he said at the time. 'And,

Villeneuve replaced Niki
Lauda at Ferrari for the
last two races of 1977,
and stayed with the team
for the rest of his career.

Gilles found himself partnering Carlos Reutemann for the final two races of the 1977 season. Lauda had already walked out, having clinched his second World Championship at Watkins Glen.

Those first two races were acutely disappointing for the Canadian. Making his Ferrari debut on home soil was not calculated to be an easy task. The Ferrari T3 steadfastly refused to warm up its Goodyear slicks in the bitterly cold conditions. He qualified well down the back and then broke a driveshaft as he attempted to spin-turn the car out of danger after a mid-race spin. The following Japanese race ended with an horrendous accident, after a collision with Ronnie Peterson's Tyrrell P34 six-wheeler. The wayward Ferrari killed two spectators who had been standing in a prohibited area.

Over the winter of 1977–78, Gilles settled down to the discipline of testing the Ferrari T2 with his team-mate Carlos Reutemann, their task considerably aided by the fact that the team had switched from Goodyear to Michelin rubber for the new season.

'When I started driving the T2, it was a bloody difficult car to drive,' he recalled with typical candour. 'The Goodyears were not so good and the Michelins made it a better car, but it was still vicious. You had to be careful with it. Maybe this was because the car had been set up for Niki. He had a certain style of driving, I suppose, and I had a different one.'

anyway, Tambay was showing almost the same promise in the Ensign which perhaps wasn't as good a car as our M23.' As things would transpire, it was the wrong decision.

Now followed something of a panic for Villeneuve. He reckoned he was good enough to bag a decent Formula 1 drive, but time was running out to get things sorted for 1978. He knew – as did everybody else in the Grand Prix paddock – that Niki Lauda would be leaving Ferrari to join Bernie Ecclestone's Brabham squad at the end of the season. But would Ferrari wait until McLaren's option expired at the end of October? Probably not. Gilles went back to Mayer to try and hurry him up. Eventually the McLaren boss relented. Yes, he could have a 'conditional release', but if Ferrart didn't snap him up then Gilles would be under option to McLaren for both 1978 and 1979. Thankfully, Ferrari was happy to do the deal and

Admittedly, even at the start of 1978, it took Gilles a couple of races to get into the swing of things. He was in a hurry to make his mark, and his fearless streak got him into situations from which he did not always have the experience to extricate himself. His great talent finally went on very public display at the 1978 Long Beach Grand Prix. He nipped through

The 1979 312T4 carried
Villeneuve and team-
mate Jody Scheckter
to three wins apiece.

Kyalami 1979. First blood for Ferrari that season went to Villeneuve, with a finely-judged win, but the French Canadian would ultimately sacrifice his Championship ambitions in favour of his more experienced team-mate.

into the lead at the first corner, and for the next 39 laps Niki Lauda and John Watson – in their Brabham BT46s – and Carlos Reutemann – in the other Ferrari 312T3 – were obliged to sit behind and watch the young superstar forging his reputation.

Sadly for Gilles, this fairy-tale progress did not run its course to the end of that race. Gilles was badly boxed-in while lapping Clay Regazzoni's Shadow DN8. On a track surface now treacherously glazed with slippery rubber and oil deposits – and his own tyres

and brakes now past their best – he made a crucial slip. Trying to squeeze past Regazzoni, he found himself vaulting over the slower car's rear wheel and spinning into a tyre barrier. Reutemann survived to give Ferrari the win that rightly belonged to Gilles.

Despite this early promise, there were those within Ferrari who doubted that Villeneuve would tidy up his act. In the aftermath of the Long Beach race, there were rumours that he would be replaced by the Italian rising star, Elio de Angelis. This speculation

Few would argue that Villeneuve was one of the most instinctive natural Racers of all time.

received added impetus when Elio won the Monaco Formula 3 supporting race in a Chevron. But, after another heroic performance in Belgium – were Gilles chased Mario Andretti's superior Lotus 79 for much of the race – the doubters kept their thoughts to themselves. Admittedly, however, Villeneuve's summer of 1978 was not as successful as he had been hoping for. Not until the Italian Grand Prix at Monza did his form with the T3 really blossom.

Monza, 1978, was the bitter race which claimed the life Ronnie Peterson. When the race was eventually restarted, Andretti and Villeneuve made the contest for the lead their own private battle, finishing 1–2 on the road. But both were penalised for jumping the start and wound up sixth and seventh; Gilles was just out of the points on Maranello's home turf. But he more than made up for that acute disappointment by rounding off the season with his maiden Grand Prix victory in the inaugural Canadian Grand Prix at Montreal, where he received his winner's trophy from the Prime Minister, Pierre Trudeau.

For 1979, Reutemann's place in the Ferrari team was taken by Jody Scheckter. After a cautious start, the two men grew to like each other and eventually became close friends. They lived quite close to each other, in Monaco, which made life easy when it came to travelling to the Ferrari track, Fiorano, for testing. But it only took a few trips as passenger in Gilles's Ferrari 308 for Jody to say instinctively: 'I'll drive' whenever they were summoned to Italy. Later, when Gilles acquired a helicopter, Scheckter's apprehension was given a further tweak. Although he had great respect for Villeneuve's ability at the controls of this

After a disappointing 1980 season with the uncompetitive T5, Villeneuve bagged two extraordinary wins in 1981 in the new turbocharged 126CK.

In 1982 both Villeneuve and Ferrari stood poised to mount a credible Championship challenge. It was not to be.

'I just couldn't believe it,' Jones said later. 'That guy would not accept that he was beaten. I sweated like hell pulling out a couple of seconds on him, relaxed a fraction through a couple of corners, and there he was in my mirrors. That red shit bucket all over me. I just had to keep running flat-out all the way to the finish because I knew if I let him past me there would be no second chance to get ahead again.'

Villeneuve attempted to out-drive Jones on every possible occasion, but there were moments when even his huge talent seemed to overstep the mark. In the 1979 Dutch Grand Prix at Zandvoort, for example, he pressed on with a deflating rear tyre until it spun him into the gravel at Tarzan. With the rubber hanging off the left-rear wheel rim, most drivers would have abandoned their car on the spot and taken the short walk back to the pits. Not Gilles. He immediately selected first gear, and drove off in search of his pits and a new wheel. The hobbled Ferrari couldn't stand the strain. Gradually, what remained of the tyre shredded itself to pieces. Then the suspension broke under the strain of being scraped along the tarmac at 100mph. By the time he got back to the pits, the left rear corner had been completely destroyed.

The real question here was whether Gilles had been a hero or a complete idiot. In purely strategic terms, one could argue that he should have taken it easily, conserved his car and come into the pits for fresh rubber at the first sign of the problem. He had, after all, been given due warning of impending trouble when he spun earlier in the race, allowing Jones through into the lead. On the other hand, there were those who marveled at his heroism and indomitable spirit. Surely this was what had inspired our interest in motor racing in the first place?

Villeneuve abided by established Ferrari team orders absolutely to the letter, supporting Scheckter all the way to the 1979 World Championship. But while Jody found himself overwhelmed by the uncompetitiveness of the 312T5 challenger in 1980, Villeneuve refused to be daunted. Highlights of his season were a climb from 23rd on the grid to fifth at the finish in Montreal, and a sensational race at Monaco where he ran on slicks in the rain.

At the end of the season, Ferrari consigned the 3-litre engine to the role of museum exhibit after no fewer than 11 seasons of Grand Prix action. It was supplanted by the first of Maranello's new 1.5-litre turbocharged V6-engines, which had originally made a tentative debut in practice for the 1980 San Marino Grand Prix. By the time Villeneuve and his new team-mate, Didier Pironi, made their racing debuts with the cars at Long Beach in 1981, the Italian team had made considerable strides in terms of throttle response and power output. But the

machine, he reckoned the Canadian pushed the edge of the performance envelope with a little too much gusto. For Jody, already toying with the idea of retirement if he won the World Championship, it was too much to live with!

The Ferrari 312T4 brought both Scheckter and Villeneuve success in fairly equal measure during 1979, but it is not for his victories at Long Beach and Kyalami that Gilles's season will be best recalled. In the French Grand Prix at Dijon-Prenois, he was embroiled in a cut-throat – and still memorable – battle for second place with Rene Arnoux's Renault turbo.

Arnoux and Villeneuve pulled out every trick in the book as they raced for the flag over the last couple of laps. To the accompaniment of endless wheel banging and locked brakes, the pair ran virtually side-by-side all the way round the final lap until Gilles, with a superhuman effort, just forced the Ferrari ahead over the final mile. Rather than erupting from their cockpits into a spontaneous brawl, the two men fell into each others arms once the race was over. Both of them knew that the other had performed to the absolute peak of his potential, every inch of the way. It was a shame that there had to be a loser.

Towards the end of the 1979 season Alan Jones, in the increasingly competitive Williams FW07, emerged as Villeneuve's prime target. The two men battled wheel-to-wheel throughout the Canadian Grand Prix, but this time Gilles had to give best to his rival.

Practice for the 1982 Belgian Grand Prix at Zolder. Villeneuve studies the time sheets and realises that his team-mate, Pironi, is quicker. His reaction was tragic.

technology involved in this new machine was crude in the extreme, epitomizing the long-held Ferrari tradition that the chassis was nothing more than an appendage onto which to hang the wheels and accommodate the driver.

Nonetheless – and certainly against the odds – Gilles notched up two of the most impressive wins of his career at the wheel of the Ferrari 126CK turbo. Having qualified an unbelievable second at Monaco, he never ran lower than third from the start and scorched past Alan Jones's Williams to take the lead in the closing stages when the Australian was slowed by fuel-feed trouble. Gilles would later describe this as the most punishing drive of his life.

'The suspension was so hard that my neck was aching badly, my head was bumping all over the place and I was having to cane the gearbox in the closing stages because the brakes were fading badly. I was pretty lucky!'

Incredibly, at the very next race, he produced another win. This time it was at Jarama, the twisting circuit outside Madrid. On this occasion he held on at the head of a close-packed train of five cars and never made a slip. With some justification, he believed that race gave him more satisfaction, from a driving viewpoint, than his Monaco triumph. 'All the time I was thinking that they could run rings round me if they wanted to,' he grinned, 'but then it was the final lap and I was still ahead.'

There was more heroism waiting down the line, but no further Grand Prix wins. He repeated his Zandvoort epic with a crazy run to third at Montreal, despite his Ferrari's front wing rearing up vertically in front of him, almost blocking his view. He later explained that he kept control by watching the right front wheel to see whether it was running on a wet or dry patch of track.

In 1982 he stayed with Ferrari, confident in his belief that Harvey Postlethwaite's engineering team could give him a competitive machine. The signs were good but, just a fortnight after Didier Pironi tricked him out of victory in the San Marino Grand Prix, Villeneue was dead – killed during practice for the Belgian Grand Prix. Trying to beat Pironi's time, Gilles had failed to lift off as he came up to lap a slower car. He was launched over its rear wheel and sent cartwheeling into the catch fencing

The day before the accident, I remember Gilles giving me his home phone number. He led me to the opposite side of the Ferrari garage – away from Pironi – for a private conversation. After the treachery of Imola, he could no longer bear to be even physically close to his team-mate. Pironi knew precisely what he was doing when he beat Villeneuve at Imola. He was deliberately unsettling the competitor whom he knew was his key rival. But even the ascetic Frenchman could never have imagined that his gamesmanship would produce such a catastrophic outcome.

Didier Pironi

THERE WAS AN AIR OF CONFIDENCE – bordering on arrogance – which suffused the character of this talented French driver, particularly towards the end of his career. That made him difficult to get close to. No matter how convivial he appeared to be on the surface, Didier Pironi always seemed to be holding something back. He did not wish to show others what he was thinking.

Born in 1952, his professional career began 20 years later, when he took sixth place in France's national Formula Renault series. This was an era of great expansion for French motor racing interests, and by 1977 Pironi had joined the long list of celebrities to have won the Monaco Formula 3 race. He was also firmly ensconced in Formula 2, so there was little surprise when Ken Tyrrell selected him to drive alongside Patrick Depailler in his Formula 1 team from the start of the 1978 season.

Tyrrell team members recall Pironi as a cool, calm and unusually controlled youngster. Yet they also remember a warm and obliging nature which perhaps became slightly concealed as he grew in stature within the motor racing community. Certainly, he took to Formula 1 like a duck to water, scoring Championship points in four of his first six races and also sharing the winning Renault at Le Mans. The French car giant was expanding its new team of Formula 1 turbo-engined cars for 1979, and wanted Pironi to sign to drive alongside Jean-Pierre Jabouille. But Ken Tyrrell had no intention of losing the services of the young driver in whom he had invested so much faith, and he refused to permit Didier the necessary contractual release.

Pironi's Formula 1 debut was with Tyrrell. This is Monaco in 1979, his second season with the team.

One season with Ligier – 1980 – saw the Frenchman score his maiden Grand Prix victory, at Zolder, and establish his reputation.

It was at Ferrari that Pironi emerged as a genuine contender – even if his ultimate potential was never completely realised.

Pironi finished four of his first six Grands Prix in the points.

The 1980 Ligier JS11 was one of the most successful of the 'ground-effect' cars.

At the wheel of the Tyrrell 009, Pironi scored his first podium finishes in 1979, with third places in the Belgian and US Grands Prix. He also put his unruffled composure on very public display when he crashed one of the Tyrrells on the fast, sweeping right-hander just before the pits at Dijon-Prenois, during practice for the French Grand Prix. The car sustained such an impact that its footwell seemed to be left connected to the rest of the chassis by a wafer-thin thread of aluminium sheeting. A quick glance at the wreckage inevitably led to fears for the driver, but the super-cool Pironi simply hopped out and strolled casually back to the pits. Not even his hair – let alone his impassive facial expression – was ruffled by what had been an extremely close shave.

He had finished 15th in the 1978 Championship, with a total of seven points for Tyrrell, and he doubled that tally the following year – moving up to tenth in the final order. But in 1980 he accepted an invitation to join Jacques Laffite in the works Ligier team, hoping that the previous season's promise displayed by its JS11 challenger would be sustained into 1980.

Ligier's development of this car, the JS11/15, produced one of the most effective members of the sliding skirt ground-effect generation. Pironi was

delighted to find his new mount gave him the chance of challenging for victory. He achieved his maiden win in the Belgian race at Zolder, out-running the Williams FW07 that Alan Jones would use to win that season's World Championship.

But that was as far as the Pironi/Ligier partnership went. The cars may have been fast, but they were highly unreliable. He managed a strong second to Jones at Paul Ricard, plus third places in South Africa, Canada and the USA. He should also have won in Montreal, but received a penalty for a jump start which allowed Jones to clinch his title with a win. He finished fifth in the Championship, but it wasn't enough for Pironi. There had never been a French World Champion in the 30-year history of that contest and Didier was absolutely determined to be the one who altered that state of affairs.

In 1981, he signed up with Ferrari. By any standards this was one hell of a challenge. Not only did he face direct comparison with the great Gilles Villeneuve, but he also arrived at Maranello just as the team was wrestling with the new turbocharged 126CK. This was not the best-handling machine, even by Ferrari standards. Frankly, Pironi struggled. At Monaco, where Villeneuve won brilliantly, the Frenchman was a lapped fourth. If one accepts that a measure of a racing driver's true genius is the form he displays in an uncompetitive car, then Pironi was not in the same league as his Canadian colleague. However, when, in 1982, the team produced the more competitive 126C2 the performance margin between the two men narrowed dramatically.

The San Marino Grand Prix at Imola represented the ultimate betrayal. Despite the chorus of disapproval

When Pironi *(left)* **broke team orders to win the San Marino Grand Prix his team-mate, Villeneuve (seen here with the legendary Ferrari engineer Mauro Forghieri) refused ever to speak to him again. Villeneuve was killed at Zolder two weeks later.**

Pironi's talent blossomed during the summer of 1982, producing a superb victory at Zandvoort and assuming the lead of the World Championship.

from the French media when this view was voiced as long ago as 1984, there is still no doubt that Pironi went out of his way to make life as uncomfortable for Villeneuve as he possibly could. Didier was a very intelligent man. He must have known that he would, on balance, find himself having to give best to Villeneuve on the circuit. So he set out to dent Gilles' confidence. He could hardly have expected to be presented with such a golden opportunity to continue this psychological warfare as that which arose during the 1982 San Marino Grand Prix.

The British Formula 1 teams, allied to the Formula One Constructors' Association, did not compete at Imola that year – for pseudo-political reasons that need not concern us here. Their absence left the spotlight falling firmly on a Ferrari–Renault battle. When the two French cars retired, Villeneuve and Pironi were left running at the front of the field in 1–2 formation. In line with established team procedure, Pironi should have stayed behind Gilles from that point onwards, but Didier kept on pulling alongside his team-mate, intent on taking his turn in the lead. Perhaps naively, Villeneuve did not seem to mind. He thought Didier was playing to the crowd, enlivening an otherwise rather dull and thinly-supported event.

But the fuel consumption of the 126C2 was extremely marginal and that worried Gilles. With this in mind, he kept the pace of the race down to around a couple of seconds a lap slower than when Pironi was in front. In retrospect, he should have been a little more wary. Although he led into the final lap, Pironi stormed through to take the win.

Pironi added insult to injury by making some extremely patronising observations about Villeneuve's driving, hinting that the Canadian was sore simply because he had been beaten fair and square. 'Losing a race is one thing,' shrugged Gilles. 'Finishing second because he steals it is quite another.'

Villeneuve's sheer indignation even struck a chord with Enzo Ferrari. In the past, il commendatore had always relished a situation where rivalry between two of his drivers had kept tension within the team bubbling along nicely. But on this occasion he felt enormous sympathy with Gilles. Part of this certainly stemmed from a genuine affection for the young French Canadian driver, part from a sense of indignation that long-established team orders should have been flouted so deliberately by Pironi. And in Ferrari's heartland, moreover, at a track which carried the name of his late son, Dino.

Ferrari had ways of signalling his feelings, usually by a well-placed and timely quote to one of the Italian newspapers. On this occasion he went out of his way to signal his disapproval of Pironi's behaviour, yet not in an overt manner. He was shrewd enough to know there was no point in marginalising the French driver who had, on this occasion, succumbed to his overwhelming competitive urge and transgressed a crucial unwritten law as a result. Pironi may have been a bastard on this occasion, reasoned Ferrari, but bastards often make the best racing drivers.

And yet, after Villeneuve's untimely death at Zolder 13 days later, there was no doubt that Pironi's talent blossomed. It was almost as if he no longer felt intimidated by the presence of his team-mate. He won the Dutch Grand Prix in magnificent style, was second in Britain and third in France. Despite this level of achievement, he was rankled by comments from certain sections of the Italian media that his Championship campaign was conducted with the attitude of a 'points gathering accountant'. These allegations needled Didier, who went into the German Grand Prix at Hockenheim in an uncharacteristically hyped-up mental state.

Irrespective of the fact that he had already clinched pole position on Friday afternoon, the Ferrari driver was running flat-out in heavy rain during Saturday morning's free practice session. In heavy spray, he ran straight into the back of Alain Prost's Renault. The Ferrari was launched into the air, landed on its tail and careered into a guard rail. By the end of its crazy journey it lay smashed at the side of the track, its driver lying in the rain-soaked wreckage with two broken legs.

This terrible smash marked the end of Didier Pironi's racing career and his ambitions of becoming France's first World Champion driver. Many operations on his legs lay ahead, but the chances of his ever returning to the cockpit of a racing car steadily receded with each passing year. Yet he had a relentless urge to find another pastime which would give him the same adrenalin buzz. Eventually he turned his hand to powerboat racing.

In the summer of 1987, competing in the Solent, he raced through the wake of a passing oil tanker without easing off on the throttle. The powerboat flipped onto its back, killing Didier Pironi and his two crew members. It was the final chapter to a tragic, tangled sequence of events.

His Championship challenge – and his Formula 1 career – was cut short by an horrific practice accident at Hockenheim in which he broke both his legs.

Nelson Piquet

NELSON PIQUET LIKED NOTHING BETTER than going to the Grand Prix grid knowing that he had a little secret, a hidden performance advantage that he had developed to give himself a leg-up on the opposition. The Brazilian driver was a great thinker, combining a cheeky and irreverent outward countenance with immense self-control and an excellent strategic mind. He was also a Racer, right enough, but only on his terms.

In 1986, upon joining the Williams–Honda squad, he was seriously displeased when he discovered his number one status merely guaranteed him priority access to the spare car. Otherwise he had to race his team-mate, Nigel Mansell, as hard as any other driver from a rival team. That was a waste of energy, reasoned Piquet. Winning races in Formula 1 is difficult enough at the best of times without having to become embroiled in competition with your team-mate, particularly when you believed the deal said otherwise. But Frank Williams, mindful of the 1981 Reutemann–Jones fiasco, would not have any of that.

And yet, even though Williams steadfastly declined to accommodate Piquet's concerns – or perhaps nobody on either side had the wit to confront them in the open – the team had absolutely no doubt about the Brazilian's ability. In testing, Mansell might inspire the mechanics with a succession of storming laps, but Piquet knew that testing was not what counted. He was always working for the race, attempting to tease something extra out of the car for the next Sunday afternoon when the starting signal was given.

Nelson was British Formula 3 top dog throughout 1978, after which he was invited to join the Brabham-Alfa squad in Formula 1. Despite a succession of problems with the Alfa Romeo-engined cars he was perfectly positioned to inherit the role of team leadership when Niki Lauda went into temporary retirement at the Canadian Grand Prix. In 1980, he scored his first Grand Prix victory, at Long Beach, and in 1981 snatched the World Championship from beneath Carlos Reutemann's nose at Las Vegas. Nelson became one of the boys, the Brabham team's mascot if you like, and he was enormously popular.

Piquet's first works Formula 1 drive was with the Brabham-Alfa team in 1979.

Runner-up to Alan Jones in the 1980 Championship, Piquet went one better in 1981 and snatched the crown from Carlo Reutemann in the last race of the year.

One of the boys: Piquet is perhaps best remembered by his many fans for his care-free days at Brabham, 1979-85.

Even by the end of 1979, Brabham's designer, Gordon Murray, admitted that he was very impressed by Piquet's talent. 'Technically I think he was improving tremendously, and there is no doubt that he learned a great deal from Niki,' said Murray. 'He wasn't afraid to make intelligent suggestions and he quickly found out what I – as an engineer – wanted to know from him. He had progressed to the point where he always provided me with intelligent, accurate and relevant information. He appreciated precisely what I needed to know in order to make progress in setting up the cars, and didn't waste any time with superfluous information.'

Nelson hadn't been unduly worried about failing to win the Championship in 1980. At the start of the 1979 season the canny Bernie Ecclestone had obtained the Brazilian's signature on a three-year contract at a bargain basement price of $50,000 a year. Admittedly, this was increased with personal appearances and some sports car driving in the BMW M1 – but it remained a cheap deal. At Montreal in 1980, Nelson made the point that if he had won that year's Championship it would not have made any difference to his retainer for the following season. By winning the Championship in 1981, however, when his initial contract was up for renewal, he was able to secure a much better deal for 1982. Nelson was certainly learning quickly from his employer.

He ran some terrific races in 1981. His victory at Buenos Aires was highly controversial, surrounded as it was over speculation as to the legality of the ride-height control system on the BT49. He then won at Imola and again, superbly, at Hockenheim, where he

parmalat
parmalat
parmalat
Santál
parmalat
GLOBO TV
Santál
Santál
MICHELIN
Ford

instantly adapted his driving style after damaging one of his Brabham's front wings against the rear of Rene Arnoux's Renault. By the end of that race, even he was beginning to admit that he was feeling pretty fortunate. The title battle went all the way to Las Vegas where his principal rival, Reutemann, seemed to capitulate. 'He braked early to let me pass when I came up behind him,' recounted an amazed Piquet. 'He made it so easy for me that I couldn't believe it.'

In 1982, Brabham switched to BMW turbo power and Nelson won just a single race. But he persevered with the new engine and was rewarded with the 1983 World Championship, a programme that was brilliantly launched with a sensational maiden victory at Rio in the all-new Gordon Murray-designed Brabham BT53.

Two relatively bleak seasons followed, but he remained loyal to Brabham until the summer of 1985, when it became clear that Ecclestone was not prepared to raise his retainer to around the $2m mark – peanuts today, but a competitive Grand Prix retainer at the time. Frank Williams, for his part, was very interested in securing the Brazilian's services as partner to Nigel Mansell, who was regarded by the team as a steady runner rather than an inspired performer.

Opposite page
Piquet's second title –
in 1983 – was his
most impressive.

Left and below
Two years with
Williams, 1986–87,
netted a third world title
but did little for his
reputation as a driver.

Frank and Nelson struck their deal in August 1995, but by the time Piquet joined the team seven months later Mansell had two Grand Prix wins under his belt and had started to emerge as a contender in his own right. It seemed as though a difficult situation was in the making. Yet Piquet could have been forgiven for thinking that the 1986 World Championship was going to be a cakewalk. Mansell tangled with Ayrton Senna's Lotus on the second lap of the Brazilian Grand Prix and Nelson won easily. But it would not be quite as simple as it seemed.

Mansell scored high profile victories in the French and British Grands Prix, but Piquet's stealthy approach began to reap dividends as he added the German and Hungarian races to his tally. He also won the Italian Grand Prix at Monza, and went into the final race at Adelaide as a Championship contender. But a precautionary pit stop, necessitated by Mansell's

high speed tyre failure, dropped him to second behind Prost. The Frenchman lucked into the World Championship.

Piquet was a great favourite with Honda, the Williams' team engine supplier, and took steps to cultivate that relationship. In 1987, he again came on strongly in the second half of the season, winning in Germany, Hungary and Italy. But he was also working the political strings to great effect. He had correctly divined Honda's dissatisfaction with Williams over the lost 1986 World Championship, and could see that a split between the two parties was imminent. With Senna – another Honda favourite – all set to move from Lotus to McLaren, Piquet played his ace card by signing a deal to replace his fellow Brazilian. This was a brilliant strategic move. It kept him in play with a top turbo engine – although not, as things transpired, a top team – and trumped Williams in the

The Brazilian saw out his Formula 1 career with the emerging Benetton team, scoring three highly lucrative victories.

same breath. Frank's team did lose its Honda deal and another five years would pass before it was a title challenger again.

Unfortunately, the move did little for Piquet either. In 1988, the Lotus 100T was hopelessly uncompetitive when ranged against the similarly-powered McLaren MP4/4s. The best Nelson could manage was third places in Brazil, San Marino and Australia. In 1989 he stayed with Lotus, now using Judd V10 engines, but he was beginning to slip down the slope to uncompetitiveness and it seemed that nothing could reverse that trend. Yet there was help at hand. Benetton threw Piquet a lifeline for the 1990 season. They had big plans for a new John Barnard-designed car, and Nelson struck a shrewd deal that would reward him on a points-related bonus system.

His 38th birthday was behind him by the time he won the Japanese Grand Prix, at Suzuka, followed by the season's finale at Melbourne. And the latter

success was certainly no Sunday afternoon drive in the country. Nigel Mansell had his Ferrari well wound up in frantic pursuit, but Nelson judged things just perfectly to scrape over the line ahead. It was a sweet triumph indeed over his old adversary. Benetton switched to Pirelli rubber in 1991. Ironically, the inconsistent performance of its tyres had been one of the reasons he abandoned Brabham at the end of 1985. But there was still one more Grand Prix victory waiting for Piquet – in Canada. It was also achieved at Mansell's expense, when the Williams driver rolled to a halt mid-way round the final lap.

The 1991 season marked the end of the road for Nelson Piquet as a Grand Prix driver. The following year he tried his hand at the Indianapolis 500, but crashed badly in practice and sustained leg injuries that effectively marked the end of his front-line career. There were still some touring car races ahead but, as a front liner, Nelson Piquet had come to the end of a long and highly successful road.

Fourteen years is a long time in Formula 1, and Piquet was at or near the top of the pile for most of that time.

133

Alain Prost

IF GOING AGAINST THE FLOW is a barometer of a sportsman's individuality and strength of character, then Alain Prost comes out pretty near the top of any list. Statistically, he is the most successful Grand Prix driver of all time, with 51 wins and four World Championships to his credit. But it is ironic that one of the greatest moments of his career – in my view – came when he withdrew from a race at the end of the opening lap.

On the face of it, one might suggest that this automatically excludes him from this volume. But, pulling out of a rain-soaked Australian Grand Prix in 1989 was a yardstick of the intelligence he applied to his motor racing; the qualities that enabled him to win all those races in the first place. As an admiring Gerhard Berger later remarked: 'We all said we would

stop after a lap, but Alain was the only man brave enough to stick to his word.'

It was Prost's final race for McLaren, as he had agreed to join Ferrari the following year. Three of his four World Championships were achieved at the wheel of a McLaren, and one for Williams – a team that he admitted did not suit him quite so well on a personal basis. In between was a stint with Ferrari that should have yielded him the 1990 title had Ayrton Senna not deliberately rammed him off the road on the first corner of the penultimate race of the season, the Japanese Grand Prix.

The thing about Prost was that he combined considerable speed with an economy of physical effort behind the wheel. He ran hard and fast, but like Niki Lauda – his teenage hero – he let the car do as much of

Nicknamed
'The Professor',
Prost combined
speed and intelligence
to become the most
successful Formula 1
driver of all time.

McLaren was
Prost's natural
home in Formula 1.

Long Beach 1981.
The Renault RE22 was
quick but unreliable.

Young blood: Prost
displayed the necessary
skills to be a Formula 1
front-runner from the
very start of his career
which, ironically, was
with McLaren, in 1980.

the work as possible. Those who believed he was a strategist more interested in gathering points than winning races were making a huge mistake. As Keke Rosberg, his McLaren team-mate in 1986, recalled: 'I thought I was the quickest driver in the world until I spent a season driving alongside Alain.' For Keke, always a great raconteur, the crucial litmus test came at Monaco, when he was running about five seconds behind Prost in second place. The Finn put in a super-human effort to clip half a second off the Frenchman's lead. 'I've got him now,' thought Rosberg, only to watch in disbelief as Alain pulled out seven-tenths of a second on him next time round. Keke knew the game was up.

Prost always performed when it really mattered. With some pride, he recounted that he'd almost always made a living out of racing, even from his early days in karting. He won the 1973 World Karting Championship, then swept all before him in the European Formula Renault and European Formula 3 championships in 1977 and 1979. That latter season also saw him win the Monaco Formula 3 classic, setting himself up for a McLaren Formula 1 test at Paul Ricard. Within three laps he was right on the pace, and Team Manager Teddy Mayer was soon rummaging through his briefcase, looking for a draft contract and a pen.

He stayed for just a single season at McLaren. The 1980 World Championship year was a troubled year for the team that had carried James Hunt to the title only four years earlier. Marlboro, its title sponsor, had become dissatisfied with its competitive level and orchestrated a merger with Ron Dennis's company, Project Four. Yet it would be 1981 before McLaren International, as the new combine was titled, exerted any significant role on the Grand Prix scene. By then Prost, unnerved by a couple of accidents clearly caused by car failure, had signed a three-year deal with Renault.

He was not destined to achieve the ambition of becoming France's first World Champion at the wheel of an all-French car. Renault's turbocharged machines were quick, but proved insufficiently reliable. In 1983 he came close, but the Championship slipped from his grasp in the closing races of the year as rivals

BMW raised the engine development stakes and provided Nelson Piquet's Brabham with more power. Renault failed to respond to this obvious challenge and lost the title at the last race. Prost was made the fall guy. Somebody had to be blamed and the Frenchman was fired. Ron Dennis, poised to return McLaren to the Formula 1 front rank thanks to the new Porsche-built TAG turbo engine, picked up Prost's services for a nominal fee. It was the driver contract bargain of the decade.

Niki Lauda had already established his position at McLaren, having made his Formula 1 comeback in 1982. But he was wary of Prost. He could see that the Frenchman was younger, more determined to make his mark. Lauda was approaching the end of his career and had a more tactical approach to gaining success. Particularly in qualifying, he saw Alain taking more risks, just as he had done ten years earlier.

McLaren was dominant in 1984. Prost scored seven wins but the title went to his wily team-mate, Niki Lauda, by just half a point.

In 1984, Prost opened the season with a psychologically crucial victory in the Brazilian Grand Prix at Rio. Lauda was on notice that the battle for the Championship would be a ferocious affair. And so it proved. The McLaren-TAG rivals carved up the season between them. Prost won seven races; Lauda five. But it was Niki who took the Championship by the slender margin of half a point.

Prost had arrived at McLaren with nine Grand Prix victories under his belt. He finished 1984 with 16 to his credit, and added another five the following year when he finally became France's first World Champion. Yet by the start of the 1986 season the McLaren-TAGs were coming under very serious pressure from the powerful Williams-Hondas, driven by Nelson Piquet and Nigel Mansell. Even so, Alain's

shrewd touch enabled him to capitalise on the intense rivalry between the Williams pair. At the final race of the season, the Australian Grand Prix, he dodged through to retain his title.

Ironically, Prost completed the final few laps of that race convinced he would not make it to the finish. He had seen first Mansell sidelined, with a 195 mph tyre failure, and then Piquet called in for a precautionary check. Alain later admitted his eyes were glued to his McLaren's fuel consumption read-out. Three laps from the end the computer was telling him that he had no fuel left, yet he survived to complete the race. It was a reversal of the situation he had experienced earlier that year, at Hockenheim, where his tanks had run dry despite the read-out showing him he had fuel to spare.

After his relationship with Ayrton Senna – his team-mate at McLaren between 1988–89 – collapsed Prost switched to Ferrari for two years.

His driving career over, Prost stayed in Formula 1 as owner and Team Manager of the Prost team (formerly Ligier).

139

After a sabbatical in 1992 Prost returned to racing for one last season – with Williams – and won his fourth World Championship title.

By 1987 the McLaren-TAG was past its best. The Williams-Hondas had the upper hand and, although Prost won three more races, he was forced to concede the World Championship to Piquet. Yet his third win that season was his 28th, making him the most successful Grand Prix driver of all-time and overtaking Jackie Stewart's record which had endured since 1973.

The 1988 season witnessed another critical sea change at McLaren. The team signed a long-term deal to use Honda turbo engines, and Ayrton Senna joined Prost to produce the most formidable line-up on the contemporary Grand Prix scene. Suddenly, Alain found himself in exactly the same situation as he had placed Niki Lauda in 1984. The dynamic Brazilian seemed prepared to risk anything in his efforts to undermine Prost's position in the team.

Nevertheless, Prost raised the standard of his game in admirable fashion. And his huge experience also played its part in narrowing the performance gap

between the two men. At Monaco, for example, Senna was half a minute ahead by the time Prost squeezed past Gerhard Berger's Ferrari into second place. Correctly judging that Ayrton's ego would prompt a response, Prost set the fastest lap of the race. Ayrton bettered it, then slid into a barrier. Although Alain had correctly read the psyche of his younger rival, he was shrewd enough to realise that he couldn't depend on slips like that from him on a regular basis.

At the end of the season Senna won the World Championship, with eight wins to Prost's seven. The two drivers continued together in 1989, but their personal relationship fell apart after Senna apparently reneged on a non-overtaking agreement on the opening lap of the San Marino Grand Prix at Imola. The relationship between the two men seemed beyond repair, and Prost decided to leave for Ferrari at the end of the season. A controversial collision between the two handed the Frenchman his third

World Championship at the season-end Japanese Grand Prix, leaving him to take the coveted number '1' to Maranello.

But Prost found himself facing more pseudo-political stress in the Italian team, where he and Nigel Mansell failed to strike up a worthwhile personal relationship. This time it was Alain who gained the upper hand, winning no fewer than five Grands Prix before Senna rammed into the back of him at Suzuka. Ferrari had not come that close to a drivers' World Championship for more than ten years. Sadly, Prost's relationship with Maranello became unravelled in 1991. Mansell had left the team at the end of the previous season and Prost found it difficult to work with the Team Manager, Cesare Fiorio. The team had a poor season and this, combined with some intemperate remarks to the media, resulted in Prost being dismissed with one race still to run that season.

He briefly toyed with the idea of racing a Ligier-Renault in 1992, going as far as to test the machine at Paul Ricard, but he wisely judged this would do nothing for his reputation. The car was quite reasonable, but certainly not a winner. He decided to sit out the year on the sidelines.

Yet Prost still wanted to race. Renault and Elf, his old partners, were keen to get him back behind the wheel of a front-running car and, in 1993, he was signed to drive a Williams-Renault. He rounded off what was to be his final season in Formula 1 with victories in the South African, San Marino, Spanish, Canadian, French, British and German Grands Prix. His new team-mate, Damon Hill, certainly put him under pressure, but Alain inevitably seemed capable of nudging the goal posts just that little bit further away each time he was seriously challenged. He retired largely because he didn't want to be partnered with Senna again in 1994. The two men even discussed it by telephone, Ayrton urging Alain that, this time, it might well work out. But Prost convinced his own rival that it really wasn't on. It was a measure of how well the two men understood each other that they could even contemplate such a private exchange of views.

Prost was at Imola when Senna died on 1 May, 1994. The signs were that the two men had reached a personal *rapprochement* and, the day before his fatal accident, Ayrton made it clear that he regarded Alain's input on any Formula 1 safety debate absolutely crucial. Others feel that, once Alain had retired, Senna suddenly appreciated just how much of his motivation had stemmed from attempting to beat the man they called 'The Professor'.

Prost's final year as a Formula 1 driver brought his career total of Grand Prix wins up to 51.

Keke Rosberg

THE 1983 BELGIAN GRAND PRIX AT SPA-Francorchamps tells you everything you need to know about Keijo 'Keke' Rosberg. Outgunned on this super-fast circuit by the more powerful turbocharged cars, the Finn – then the reigning World Champion – drove the wheels off his Williams FW08C to finish fifth, the first naturally-aspirated car to cross the line. Rosberg caned that car to within a few inches of its life in a characteristic display of over-the-top commitment and determination. Indeed, those qualities were on regular display that season. Think of Long Beach, where he spun through 360 degrees on the opening lap and still retained his position. Or of Monaco, where he started a damp race on slicks and delivered an audacious performance to score only the second Grand Prix win of his career.

Rosberg gained his early motor racing experience in Formula Vee single seaters, before making a name for himself in Formula 2 and emerging a surprise winner of the rain-soaked 1978 International Trophy at Silverstone. In 1980–1981 he drove for the Fittipaldi team, but its star was fading fast and he decided to leave mid-way through the second season. Nevertheless, he had made a sufficient impression to be selected for a Williams test at Paul Ricard once Alan Jones had announced his retirement. Rosberg proved to be an absolute revelation.

Initially, he was expected to take the number two role as team-mate to Carlos Reutemann, but when the Argentine driver quit the sport after only two races the Flying Finn was propelled into the team leadership, a role he fulfilled with enormous relish. To win the 1982 World Championship at the wheel of the Cosworth-engined Williams FW08 was quite an achievement. He drove his heart out from the start of the year and, although he only won a single Grand Prix, that achievement should be set against an unusual season in which no driver managed more than two victories.

'Sure, it was frustrating not having a turbo,' he recalled. 'But there was no point complaining about it. Anyway, as I think I proved when I put the FW08 on pole position for the British Grand Prix at Brands Hatch, a Cosworth car could be competitive on all but the fastest circuits.'

Despite his terrific bravado, his opposite-lock style frustrated Williams' outspoken Technical Director, Patrick Head: 'I've told Keke that if only he tidied up his driving style, he would be even quicker than he is.' Rosberg, never one to be cowed, responded robustly to this line of thinking: 'I drive that way because that's how I like it, and it seems to work pretty well.' Rosberg was also a heavy smoker, a habit that drove Frank Williams to distraction. Frank would

Rosberg was propelled into the Williams' team leadership after Reutemann's sudden retirement.

With his wife, Sina.

Rosberg, pictured here during his final season, had a style both on and off the track that was unorthodox, and followed in the finest traditions of great Scandinavian drivers such as Peterson.

never allow him to smoke in the motorhome, so Keke could often be seen furtively puffing outside its door, looking for all the world like a schoolboy caught with a packet of Woodbines behind the bike sheds. Indeed, Williams once made the mistake of attributing Keke's occasional first lap slips to a lack of physical stamina. 'Bullshit,' retorted the Finn. 'We used to start the races with low tyre pressures so that they came up to precisely the correct temperature when they warmed up. It was necessary to manhandle the car on the opening lap because it was extremely twitchy until the tyres came up to pressure.'

Keke was proud of the fact that he always raced flat-out to the finish of his races. Getting a dig in at his rival Nelson Piquet after finishing second to the exhausted Brazilian at Rio in 1982, he added: 'Anyway, I'm not the one who faints after a race.'

Having won the 1982 title, Keke admitted that he was probably at the point faster than at any other moment in his career. 'I just wasn't prepared to accept that anybody could beat me, and was prepared to take massive risks to stay with the turbos,' he remembers. 'I loved every minute of it.'

By 1984, Williams had climbed aboard the turbo bandwagon with Honda. The business of integrating chassis and engine into a totally new package was complex, and involved a certain amount of trial and error. There was no data bank of previous experience to draw upon and the Williams FW09 development was very much a trip into the unknown. Under these sorts of circumstances, it was just the job to have Rosberg's versatility on tap. Sure enough he criticised

KEKE ROSBERG

the FW09's shortcomings, but he gave it 100% every time he sat behind the wheel, and it was no surprise when he posted its maiden victory in the sweltering heat of Dallas, Texas, in June 1984.

The major controversy of that weekend centred round whether the new track surface would survive the stresses and strains of a complete race. Even when the cars lined up on the starting grid there were several competitors who believed that it would be flagged to a halt after a handful of laps. But Keke, who had invested $2,500 in a water-cooled skullcap to wear beneath his helmet, knew otherwise. By the end of the afternoon his purchase was to look like the bargain of the decade. As the race unfolded, so Keke gradually picked up the pace. He was always at his best in the role of Formula 1's great improviser, ready to deal with the unpredictable variables of even the most torrid conditions. After breaking clear of a battle with Nigel Mansell's Lotus, Rosberg went on to win the race in splendid style.

At this stage in his career, Rosberg had his personal enthusiasm for Nigel Mansell well under control, and he was deeply concerned when Frank Williams indicated that he would be signing the British driver for the 1985 season. Worried about Mansell's perceived reputation as a disruptive influence, Keke asked Frank to reconsider. If he did not, warned the Finn, then he would be leaving the team at the end of the following season, when his contract expired. Frank didn't reconsider; Keke left the team. That said,

Rosberg would later confess that Mansell was far less trouble than he had expected. The two drivers were now armed with the superb, much improved Williams FW10 – the first carbon-fibre chassis to be produced by Patrick Head's design team – and the drivers won two races each.

But it was Rosberg's sensational 160mph pole winning lap at Silverstone, harnessing every ounce of the 1100bhp developed by his Honda turbo, that really stuck in the mind. Keke had waited patiently in the pit lane for what he judged the right moment, stubbed his cigarette out beneath the heel of his racing boot and said: 'OK, let's do it.' The fact that a slow puncture was detected on his return to the pit lane was a footnote that simply added to the enormity of the Finn's achievement.

By the end of his four-year partnership with his team, Frank Williams believed that Rosberg had matured enormously as a professional racing driver and had also become more technically competent.

'He realised that he had to think a lot more about the business of being a Grand Prix driver,' said Williams. 'And he really began to flourish as he did more testing and accumulated more experience. He was unquestionably very intelligent, but I always felt that to some extent he short-changed himself, because he never spent anywhere near long enough in (technical) de-briefs. Twenty minutes, and he was off.

'He could also be very impatient, particularly with Honda, but he always had great judgement on tyres. He invariably managed to select the best compounds

Rosberg joined the reigning World Champion, Alain Prost, at McLaren in 1986. He retired at the end of the year after a largely disappointing season.

Running on empty: the 1986 fuel consumption regulations did not suit Rosberg's foot-to-the-floor driving style.

just by feel. He had brilliant car control, but not in a rock-ape manner – he was too clever for that. Again, like Carlos Reutemann, if Patrick and I had given him more personal attention then I think he would have liked that.'

During the 1985 season, he won the Detroit and Australian Grands Prix. In his own mind he believed that he should also have won in South Africa, but a lurid slide on some dropped oil lost him crucial time early in the race.

His final Grand Prix season, at the wheel of a McLaren-TAG, proved to be extremely frustrating. He took part in all 16 races, but only finished five of them. The restrictions on fuel capacity and turbo boost pressure meant that Grands Prix were more akin to economy runs, with those who eked out the fuel allowance to best effect emerging on top. This was definitely not up Rosberg's street: 'I could neither accept nor understand that Formula 1 cars could not – and were not allowed to – carry enough fuel to go flat-out,' he pondered. 'It was against my system.' He also found it very difficult to adapt his driving technique to get the best out of a McLaren-TAG that was tailored to Alain Prost's preference for a touch of understeer.

Yet he enjoyed his time driving for Ron Dennis. It was an experience that he'd heard so much about from others and wanted to sample for himself. They obviously got on well enough, since Rosberg went on to manage Dennis protégé – and Finland's second World Champion – Mika Hakkinen.

145

Nigel Mansell

NIGEL MANSELL WAS A PHENOMENON. You could like him; you could loathe him. But there was certainly no way you could ignore him. He was one of the most visually exciting drivers of his era, with considerable ability and more determination than most of his rivals put together. He was also

enormously brave, as his exploits on high-speed circuits in a succession of Williams-Honda, Ferrari and Williams-Renault cars repeatedly demonstrated.

He could also be an extraordinarily tricky customer to deal with. Because he had total faith in his own ability, he was a man who drove astonishingly hard bargains with all the teams for whom he drove, leaving them shaken and whimpering financially. Yet perhaps the most astonishing thing about these negotiations was that, no matter how bitterly his teams complained off-the-record, the deal was inevitably done. It had to be, because he was a bums-on-seats, box office star.

Sometimes, he could demonstrate an unexpectedly wry sense of humour. I recall him sitting on the rear wheel of his Lotus, with his wife Rosanne, in the Kyalami pit lane during the 1982 South African Grand Prix meeting. A dispute between drivers, team owners and the FIA over the terms of the new drivers' 'super licence' had thrown doubt over not only that individual race, but also the whole future of the World Championship. Seeing his Grand Prix career going down the pan even before it had properly started, Nigel commented: 'Well, Rosanne, it looks like it's back to working for British Gas for you, doesn't it?' Happily for an army of fans who would grow to support him across the world, this would not be the case. But his talent was not universally recognised at this early stage in his career, although it has to be acknowledged that the Lotus boss, Colin Chapman, certainly believed he had the spark.

Mansell came up the hard way, and seized every opportunity that presented itself. In 1979, he was invited to join a Formula 1 test with Lotus at Paul Ricard. It was a break he would not miss for the world. Despite suffering with a cracked vertebra sustained during a Formula 3 collision at Oulton Park, Mansell was on his way. He made the trip and, munching painkillers like chocolate drops, never allowed anybody an inkling of his physical dilemma. Chapman was impressed, signing him on as test driver. The Lotus chief also gave him his Grand Prix debut at the Österreichring the following year, where he manhandled the spare Type 81 onto last place on

the grid. The fact that the car sprang a fuel leak into the cockpit just prior to the start didn't bother Nigel. He drove as hard as he could until the engine failed. When he finished the race his hamstrings were so shrunken by their dousing in petrol that he could hardly walk.

He was promoted to the Lotus race team in 1981 and Chapman doubled his retainer when he finished third in the Belgian Grand Prix at Zolder. Later in the season he finished a strong fourth at Caesars Palace, but that was the sum total of his achievements that year. Even so, he was optimistic that 1982 would be different.

It wasn't. The only Lotus victory fell to his teammate, Elio de Angelis, in a photo-finish with Keke Rosberg's Williams at the Österreichring. The entire team was felled by bitter tragedy when Chapman died suddenly in December 1982. Mansell had lost his patron and Lotus Team Manager Peter Warr, who continued running the team for many years, was certainly not an unqualified fan of the confident young English driver.

Nevertheless, the 1984 season saw Nigel coming closer than ever to scoring his first Grand Prix win for Lotus. He was leading in the pouring rain at Monaco when he lost adhesion on a painted road marking and

Four seasons with the Norfolk team promised much but failed to produce that elusive first win.

The move to Williams in 1985 marked a turning point in Mansell's career.

149

slid into a barrier. Warr reckoned he had squandered his opportunity, and his future career prospects with Lotus were looking bleak. It was pretty clear that Mansell and Lotus were not going to stay together beyond the end of the year. Yet Frank Williams had been impressed with Nigel's gritty style and offered him a deal which effectively saved his career. 'Frank picked me up when I was nothing,' said Mansell later. But over the years that followed he would repay Williams's faith, with interest.

He was beyond the straightforwardly brave. He raced at Silverstone in the 1985 British Grand Prix only a week after slamming off the road at 190mph during practice at Paul Ricard. Only a few months later, he brought the crowds to their feet with a rousing victory in the Grand Prix of Europe at Brands Hatch. He had given the fans the first win by a British driver since John Watson four years earlier. He became a national hero almost overnight.

But, for all this enthusiasm, Mansell was still cast in the number two role for the 1986 season, as Williams running mate to Nelson Piquet. Yet Nigel was able to undermine the Brazilian's confidence with a succession of superb wins in Belgium, Canada, France, Britain and Portugal. Everything he did seemed to be tinged with a bit of theatre. Even unconsciously he was the centre of attention, and at the wheel it was high drama stuff – win or bust. During the 1986 Australian Grand Prix, for example, a 190mph tyre failure wrote *finis* to his Championship hopes, yet such was the level of confidence he

was displaying nobody could have imagined it would take six long years before he bagged the world title for himself.

Twice during that period, first at Brands Hatch and then again at Silverstone the following year, Mansell and Piquet battled it out head-to-head, and on both occasions Nigel emerged triumphant. That Silverstone performance, 1987, was possibly the greatest drive of his career, a stupendous recovery from a mid-race tyre stop which saw him make up half a minute and overtake Piquet on the penultimate lap. To add to the drama, his car ran out of fuel on the slowing down lap. And he kissed the track surface at the point where he had outfumbled the Brazilian.

Piquet won the Championship and quit the team. Nigel's title hopes ended with a huge shunt during practice for the Japanese Grand Prix, forcing him to miss the final two races of the year. It also left him struggling with Judd V8 engines for 1988. Then Mansell, too, decided to leave – intoxicated by the lure of Ferrari. If the truth be told, he was just the sort of guy for Maranello, and it didn't take long before he was dubbed 'Il Leone'. He made himself an Italian hero with a fortuitous victory in the first race of 1989, the Brazilian Grand Prix.

He stayed with the team for two turbulent seasons. As usual, he was either at the centre of the action or stirring up the controversy. He drove brilliantly to outfox Ayrton Senna and win the 1989 Hungarian Grand Prix, but also found himself suspended for one race after reversing in the pit lane during a Portuguese Grand Prix pit stop when well in the lead and ignoring the black flag.

In 1990, Alain Prost joined Ferrari and everything began to go wrong for Mansell. His car suffered much more in the way of mechanical unreliability and Nigel began to have suspicions that he and Prost were not playing on an even field. Finally, after he retired with gearbox problems from the British Grand Prix at Silverstone, he decided he would retire at the end of the season. 'The hardest decision of my life,' was how he described it. So Ferrari made arrangements for Jean Alesi to replace him in 1991, only for Mansell to reverse his retirement decision and accept an offer to return to Williams. Now 36 years old, he wanted that World Championship more than ever and was convinced that the Williams-Renault partnership was now capable of delivering it.

His judgement was absolutely on the button. The new Williams FW14 was certainly a sensational car, equipped with a reliable engine, active suspension, semi-automatic gearbox and traction control. Yet it was not sufficiently reliable for Nigel to clinch that year's Championship. For that he would have to wait until the following season.

'Il Leone': Mansell's gritty style made him an instant favourite with the *tifosi*.

As team-mate to Prost in 1990, Mansell's relationship with Maranello began to disintegrate.

From the start of the 1992 season nothing could touch the Williams-Renault FW14B, and Mansell became the first driver ever to win the first five races in any season. He clinched the title as early as the Hungarian Grand Prix, in August, and then topped that with an all-time record ninth win (in Portugal) in one season. There could be no doubt that he was driving at peak form, extracting every ounce of potential from what was unquestionably the best car in the field. But Frank Williams was nurturing a problem. He was being encouraged by Elf and Renault to sign Alain Prost for 1993, and he knew that Mansell would not be keen on the news. Eventually, however, he agreed nearly £1m additional financial compensation for Mansell to relinquish his absolute number one status. Amazingly, Mansell and Williams then fell out over

the number of hotel rooms the team would provide for Nigel's family in 1993. Before any outsiders could sit them both down and bang their heads together Nigel had announced that he would retire from Formula 1 at the end of the season.

This time he really meant it and, within a few weeks, it was confirmed that he would drive in the US domestic CART series the following year, at the wheel of a Newman-Haas Team Lola-Ford. The American adventure was a typical Mansell-style, bells-and-whistles affair. He may have been nudging 40, but his racer's instinct immediately came to the fore. Testing at the Phoenix oval circuit he slammed backwards into the wall at 170mph, painfully damaging blood vessels deep in his back. He recovered superbly to finish third at his first try in the Indianapolis 500 – and almost won outright.

Finishing the 1993 season as CART Champion, he was determined to hold onto that title the following year. But the Lola-Ford was no longer as crisply competitive as it had been the previous season and Mansell's head was turned by a huge Renault-funded offer to return to Formula 1 on a guest basis with Williams. For a fee rumoured to be around £1m per race, he accepted the invitation to drive in four Grands Prix. He retired from two, finished fourth at Suzuka, and then rounded off the season with victory – his 31st – in the Australian Grand Prix after Schumacher and Hill eliminated themselves in a controversial collision.

But, for the 1995 season Williams preferred to retain the young Scot, David Coulthard, and Mansell was suddenly on the market again. His decision to sign for McLaren looked questionable, to say the least. Now turned 40, Mansell was only interested in putting his reputation on the line at the wheel of a fully competitive car. The McLaren-Mercedes partnership had still to be developed to a winning pitch, and both parties should have recognised this earlier. The fiasco ended with a premature, mutually agreed termination of the deal. Both McLaren and Mansell should have known better.

A lucrative return to Williams for four races in 1994 saw his last – and 31st – Grand Prix win, at Adelaide.

A Karate black belt and professional-standard golfer, Mansell was always a highly versatile sportsman.

155

Ayrton Senna

AYRTON SENNA'S DEATH WAS AN EVENT OF seismic proportions. Like the assassination of President Kennedy, it was a moment when life seemed to stand still. In motor racing terms, only Jim Clark's fatal accident, 26 years earlier, had been received with the same overwhelming sense of grief.

Yet times had changed dramatically during that intervening generation. Whereas Clark crashed virtually without a witness, Senna's accident was played out on prime time global television. Countless fans across the world found themselves unwittingly intruding into the final moments of the man who many regarded as the greatest sporting hero of all time.

In many ways, Senna was a child of the media generation. Had he raced in Clark's time he would have been hailed for his driving genius alone. But in a more pushy era, when the media felt it was now its right to probe and investigate, the Brazilian was unmasked as a ferociously motivated competitor who quite obviously believed he could do no wrong.

And whereas Clark had seemed inviolate, a man who always kept something in hand, Senna was a driver who operated on the absolute limit from the first to the last lap of his career. Winning was just not sufficient for this enigmatic genius from São Paolo. He needed to dominate not only the races, but every qualifying and test session as well.

When he died he had achieved 41 Grand Prix victories, placing him second behind Alain Prost in the all-time winners' stakes. His 65 pole positions perhaps represent a more compelling indicator of what made him tick. He was also World Champion in 1988, 1990 and 1991, each time at the wheel of a McLaren-Honda.

It was Senna's absolute refusal to compromise that remained the single most remarkable element of his character. And this did not simply apply out on the circuit. When contract negotiation time arrived with whichever of the four teams – Toleman, Lotus, McLaren or Williams – he drove for during his career,

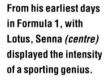

From his earliest days in Formula 1, with Lotus, Senna *(centre)* displayed the intensity of a sporting genius.

Three years with
Lotus established
his reputation.

The McLaren
years underlined
his brilliance.

their company lawyers took a deep breath and braced themselves. They knew full well that they would be required to earn their money as seldom before while Senna and his advisors went through each and every clause of the proposed agreement in precise and meticulous detail. He was supremely intelligent, with a calculating mind that could always work out a way of resolving problems to his own best advantage. Yet there was also a defensive streak to his personality, as though he expected people to be critical of him before they actually were.

Family values meant an enormous amount to him, perhaps second only to his religious beliefs, but he was not a man who would take you into his confidence and share with you his personal philosophy, as it applied either to life in general or motor racing in particular. I am also tempted to say that he was not always a good sportsman.

The son of a wealthy Brazilian businessman, Senna displayed his independence almost from the start of his European single-seater career. At the end of 1981, he was prepared to abandon his racing career after only a season of Formula Ford, indignant that the commercial realities of life meant that he still had to produce sponsorship if he wanted to continue racing the following year. In Ayrton's view, merit alone should have been sufficient.

Yet he was bold in his dealings with the top teams. In 1983, McLaren offered to fund Senna's British Formula 3 Championship programme in exchange for an option on his services. Many youngsters in that position would

Flawed genius?
One could argue that
Senna's self-belief
clouded his judgement.

Previous pages
Monaco, 1984.
Darkening skies herald
a rainstorm that would
expose Senna's extra-
ordinary skill to the
world for the first time.
He finished second in
the Toleman, behind
Prost, and would
certainly have won
had the race not
been stopped early.

have jumped at such an opportunity, but Ayrton declined politely. He told Ron Dennis that he would generate his own finance, thanks very much, which would also enable him to retain his independence and keep all his options open. It was a disarmingly confident strategy for a 23-year-old to adopt.

Senna graduated into Formula 1 with Toleman after winning the 1983 Formula 3 title that, rather ironically, earned him a test drive with McLaren. The Toleman team was instantly won over by the brilliant young Brazilian. At the wheel of their Hart turbo-engined TG184, he finished second at Monaco and third – beaten only by the McLarens of Prost and Lauda – in Portugal. Yet such was his talent that everybody at Toleman realised he would quickly outgrow the team and the modest resources it could deploy to his advantage. Brian Hart, in particular, was stunned at the way in which he came to grips with the specialised technique of driving a turbo-charged Formula 1 car.

On one occasion Hart recalled Senna carrying out fuel mixture control tests at Brands Hatch, and his feel for the engine's response absolutely corroborated what the engineers discovered on the test bed.

He also surprised Hart by telling him that he did not use the rev counter, only the turbo boost gauge: 'I use the rev counter perhaps for fifth to sixth,' explained Ayrton. 'But in all the other gears I just wait until the boost gauge is at the right point – and I can feel the engine struggling a bit – and I stick it into the next gear.'

Senna switched to Lotus the following year and his first Grand Prix victory soon followed – only the second race of the season – in the pouring rain at Estoril. This hypnotic demonstration of high speed car control was followed by five more Lotus victories over the next three seasons, but it wasn't until he joined the McLaren squad at the start of 1988 that he seriously put an arm lock on the Grand Prix winner's circle.

Few drivers in history have ever applied so much mental focus to the business of Formula 1. Ayrton was forever probing, exploring and analysing ways in which he could gain an edge. Indeed, it took him little over a season of intense psychological warfare to unseat Alain Prost from his position at McLaren, driving him into the arms of the rival Ferrari camp.

His attitude towards Prost, nursed during their second year together at McLaren and allowed to worsen thereafter, was seen by many as nothing more than a reflection of Senna's competitive spirit. I always believed it was irrational and, if anything, it devalued Senna's position among the ranks of the all-time great racing drivers. It was also the view of many colleagues that he not only lacked a sense of humour, but also a degree of perspective. He almost exclusively reserved the former for his close friends, who came from in or around his immediate family.

Yet the tensions that grew between Prost and Senna during 1988–89 were, to some extent, inevitable.

McLaren provided the
tools with which the
Brazilian could realise
his ultimate ambitions.

Donington 1993: yet
another memorable
victory for the wet
weather wizard.

Senna's last race for McLaren, the Australian Grand Prix of 1993, was also his last Grand Prix victory.

A rare moment of relaxation: Senna celebrates winning the 1991 World Championship at a Honda party.

Prost wanted to protect his position; Senna to undermine it. You could see Alain's point of view. He had been the rock upon which much of McLaren's success had been built, and now the balance of power was shifting in Senna's favour.

Out on the circuit, he displayed absolutely decisiveness. If anything, his consummate skill unleashed an overconfidence that produced the occasional accident, but usually resulted in Grand Prix victory. Yet he simply could not accept defeat. A classic example of this was the manner in which he rammed Prost's Ferrari off the circuit on the first corner of the Japanese Grand Prix, in 1990, after being frustrated in his attempt to move pole position to the other side of the circuit. The episode suggested that Senna's messianic zeal might extend to discarding considerations of his own personal safety, let alone those of anybody else on the circuit.

Of course there was an enormous paradox to all this. To his handful of close friends – such as McLaren Team Co-ordinator Jo Ramirez and Formula 1 medical expert Professor Sid Watkins – he displayed humour, generosity and huge personal warmth. Ramirez first met him at Silverstone in 1981. He was at a test session with the Fittipaldi team when Emerson Fittipaldi brought along a shy youngster.

Imola, 1994. Senna's tenure at Williams was cut tragically short.

'Ayrton had come to talk to Emerson,' remembers Ramirez. 'And when he left, Emerson told me that I had just met the guy who would be one of the greatest drivers of all one day. After that I followed Ayrton's career very closely.' Ramirez was one of the few individuals who retained the close respect and affection of both Prost and Senna. Sometimes it was no easy balancing act, but the quiet Mexican's overwhelming good nature always won the day.

The difference between the two drivers was that Alain, in a car set up especially for him, was untouchable. Unbeatable, perhaps. But Ayrton could drive anything, no matter how badly it was handling. That was certainly the case in Senna's final race. The Williams FW16 was probably not a car that should have been on pole position at that stage in its development. It was there because Ayrton was driving it. Michael Schumacher, whose Benetton was following Senna in the early stages, later said that he could see the Brazilian was having problems with his car. But Ayrton was never a man to take it easy.

Professor Sid Watkins was another who was close to Ayrton: 'I admired his humility, his humour and his kindness – not on the track, perhaps, but off,' he said. 'I also found him to be a very sincere person. He would always be one of the first to ring up if anybody was sick or injured to ask if he could help.'

Gerhard Berger, who drove with Senna at McLaren for three seasons from 1990, judged the whole affair a unique experience. He saw enough to convince himself that Senna had crafted McLaren into his own personal team and told Ron Dennis as much. The

McLaren chief had wanted Gerhard to stay into 1993, but the Austrian wasn't interested. Not while Ayrton was there. Yet while he was unable to match Senna on the circuit, he certainly helped the Brazilian lighten his mood, exposing a sense of humour which perhaps even Ayrton himself hadn't realised he possessed.

'On one occasion,' remembers Berger, 'we were sitting in a traffic jam in Milan – I was driving – and Ayrton pulls the keys out of the ignition and throws them out into the road. He had clearly forgotten that he was Ayrton Senna, I was Gerhard Berger, and we were in the middle of Milan. When we climbed out to try and find the keys, the whole of the city seemed to come to a halt. Eventually the police had to rescue us by helicopter. They were not amused.'

This happy tale reminds us of Ayrton's human side, one that he chose so often to conceal from view. He was a difficult man, but a great sportsman in his chosen sphere. He could be awkward and confrontational, yet perhaps this was part of the driving force which made him such a great driver.

Was he the greatest that ever lived? Probably. But then it is almost impossible to compare drivers of different generations. Many of the mechanics and engineers who worked with him have few doubts on this score. They were inspired and motivated by the sheer force of his personality and talent. When he died, contemporary Grand Prix racing lost a touch of its magic. How long would he have raced? As long as he thought he was not losing his touch. But he would have realised – and retired – long before anybody else had even started to notice.

Michael Schumacher

IT IS A GRAPHIC REMINDER OF THE MILLIONS of pounds involved in contemporary Grand Prix motor racing that, when Michael Schumacher traded up to a sleek Challenger private jet in 1998, his manager, Willi Weber, purchased the Cessna Citation plane which the Ferrari ace was discarding. It was an exchange that raised the prospect of the Formula 1 manager as someone rich enough to require his own manager. Yet if Weber, a well-groomed Stuttgart-based entrepreneur, can afford his own wings, then he has certainly earned the privilege. If you take Schumacher's genius at the wheel out of the equation, then it is the 54-year-old Weber who has been responsible for the German driver's rise to fame and fortune.

Nevertheless, by the end of the 1998 season the 29-year-old Ferrari driver had amassed 33 Grand Prix victories. That put him just eight away from Ayrton Senna's tally of 41, and a more challenging 18 away from Alain Prost's all-time record. Even so, it would

be a brave man indeed who would bet against him passing both these distinguished milestones before he finally calls it a day.

At home in Germany, Michael rides on a tidal wave of popular support, the like of which far surpasses the adulation shown towards fellow German sporting legends such as Boris Becker and Jürgen Klinsmann. Even the controversy at Jerez in 1997, where he rammed his Ferrari into the side of Jacques Villeneuve's Williams in a manoeuvre that was universally condemned as a professional foul, failed materially to dent his popularity. There was a brief period of criticism, but Schumacher quickly regained his status in the eyes of the fans. His so-called punishment, of being disqualified from second place in the World Championship, carried with it an obligation to help with a European road safety campaign backed by motor racing's governing body, the FIA. It proved to be an exercise that was deftly turned into something of a public relations triumph for the Ferrari driver.

Having made his Formula 1 debut with Jordan, Schumacher was snapped up by Benetton and displayed exceptional promise from the outset.

Opposite page
Schmacher enjoys massive support among his own countrymen.

The Benetton team was built around Schumacher during 1992–93.

Opposite top and bottom
The reward came over the next two years, 1994–95, when the team netted 19 victories, two drivers' championships and one constructors' title.

Yet there is something compelling about the little boy lost demeanour of this lad from the wrong side of the tracks who has made 'The Big Time'. His father was a bricklayer; his mother ran the hamburger stand at the go-kart track in Kerpen, where the young Michael first cut his competitive teeth. He may seem surly and uninterested when faced with one of the obligatory press conferences which take place daily at each Grand Prix. He might duck questions, or reply with sweeping and anodyne generalities. But on his own, Schumacher is better value. Like the late Ayrton Senna, he weighs his replies carefully behind a mask of slightly distant formality. As his team-mate at Ferrari, Eddie Irvine, says: 'Michael is always pretty intense. There is nothing lighthearted about Grand

Prix racing for him. He is there to win and nothing else.' Small talk with the press is a necessary inconvenience, but he carries it off cordially enough.

In 1989, Weber recruited the young Michael Schumacher to drive for his own Formula 3 team, and the two men have never looked back, earning riches beyond their wildest dreams. It was Schumacher's third place in that year's German Formula 3 championship that put him on the map. Thanks to these performances, Weber was able to negotiate a deal for him to join the Mercedes-Benz sports car racing team where, together with Karl Wendlinger and Heinz-Harald Frentzen, they were promoted as German's new generation of racing stars. Schumacher trusts Weber's judgement completely. 'If they have a new

sponsor, Willi will do all the negotiations,' says an insider. 'If the terms seem to Willi's liking, he will then present them to Michael.

'This is a serious partnership. They are business colleagues and close friends. Willi knows that his main priority is to take all the worries off Michael's shoulders. It is very important that he has his mind free for what he does best: the racing.'

Such a division of labour clearly works well. Weber's assiduous dealings should ensure that his driver earns around $125m from retainers and marketing agreements under the terms of his latest Ferrari contract, which lasts through to the end of 2002. Less Weber's commission, of course, which is put at around 20%.

Ironically, it seems that Schumacher may never drive a Mercedes-powered car in Formula 1. Stuttgart insiders hint that he carries a little too much controversial baggage with him. The collision with Damon Hill which resolved the 1994 World Championship is one example; the incident with Villeneuve at Jerez another. By contrast, Ferrari wants the very best driver available and is prepared to put up with everything to keep him. Under such circumstances, it is quite understandable that the Maranello team is prepared to accept Michael's requirement that they sign a number two driver who is prepared to play second fiddle. That said, Irvine has proved to be both a Grand Prix winner and a solid team player, who admits that only occasionally does he feel he can match Schumacher's absolute speed.

Right and below
The move to Ferrari
in 1996 represented
the ultimate challenge
for the German. It
also made him one of
the richest sportsmen
in history.

It is 20 years since Jody Scheckter clinched the last drivers' World Championship at the wheel of a Ferrari, leading his team-mate, Gilles Villeneuve, across the line at Monza to win the Italian Grand Prix. Ironically, team orders also played a part in the outcome of that particular race, albeit in a subtly different manner.

In those days, Ferrari standing orders required that the drivers should not race each other once they assumed first and second places at the head of the field. But it was the team owners who called the shots. Enzo Ferrari bestrode the Grand Prix world like an irascible automotive colossus, paying his star drivers a few hundred dollars a month and invariably heightening the tension between them by failing to nominate a team leader. In the era of Michael Schumacher, the best driver in the world dictates the terms at Ferrari. He knows how difficult it really is to win a World Championship, and does not intend to let the interests of his team-mate get in the way of his own ambition.

Schumacher burst on the Grand Prix scene in the summer of 1991, when he was invited to test at Silverstone for the Jordan team.

'It was instantly clear that Michael was very special,' remembers Eddie Jordan. 'We tested him on the south circuit at Silverstone, which in those days was a fairly hair-raising place. Within a few laps he was braking 15 metres later for the kink before the pits than anybody else who had previously driven the car. We were signalling to come in because we thought he was going too quickly too soon. But he knew what he was doing. Within five minutes we were convinced that he was pretty special.'

Ken Tyrrell recognised the same sort of natural talent in Schumacher that he had seen in Jackie Stewart 30 years before. 'It is that terrific ability to put in a quick

Like Ayrton Senna, Schumacher has driven some spectacular races in the wet – such as Monaco, 1997.

169

Search for a star: Schumacher filled the void created by the sudden death of Ayrton Senna.

first lap at the start of a race,' he said. 'Stewart was exactly the same, easily the best of his generation.'

After only one race for Jordan in 1991, Michael switched to the Benetton team under controversial circumstances. For several years thereafter, Jordan would argue that this was a major breach of contract. The matter was eventually settled amicably, and away from the public gaze. Schumacher won his first Grand Prix, at Spa-Francorchamps, for Benetton in 1992. His next came at Estoril the following year. But in 1994, equipped with the superb Benetton-Ford B194, he was set to run away with the title. In fact, he was dogged by a seeming endless run of controversy. Excluded from both the British and Belgian Grand Prix and suspended from Italy and Portugal, he still hung on to win the title by a single point. But the manner in which he clinched the Championship – by bundling Damon Hill off the road in Adelaide – has always coloured his achievement in the minds of many Formula 1 insiders.

In 1995, Benetton switched to Renault power and Michael won his second Championship in rather more decisive fashion. His switch to Ferrari came at a time when the Italian team was in the middle of a high profile recovery programme under the steward-ship of the former Peugeot sports car chief, Jean Todt. Michael's first Ferrari victory was in the pouring rain at Barcelona in 1996. He followed that up with two fine wins at Spa and Monza, but the Ferrari didn't consistently come onto the pace until the second half of the year. It was too late to mount a title challenge, but the omens were certainly promising for 1997.

Luca di Montezemolo, Ferrari's Chairman, made it the team's priority to win more races in 1997 than they had the previous year. Michael duly deliv-ered, almost doubling the tally to five. But then came the vital fumble at Jerez, handing Villeneuve the Championship and leaving Michael facing more criticism and doubt.

Surely, 1998 had to be the year in which the Championship went Ferrari's way. Michael had six wins under his belt by the time he lined up on pole position at Suzuka, and it was an even call whether or not he would finally get the job done for Maranello. Then, at the first re-start, his engine stalled. It was an episode that served as a reminder that even the greatest drivers are still human. He was consigned to the back of the grid, and ultimately retired with a punctured tyre – leaving McLaren's Mika Hakkinen to win both the race and the World Championship.

Yet again, Michael had proved himself to be suffused with a dazzling talent – an almost magical touch – behind the wheel. Yet, like the late Ayrton Senna, whose mantle he has now assumed, he displays an arrogance and intolerance of others. When he bundled Heinz-Harald Frentzen's Williams off the road during the 1998 Canadian Grand Prix, he could scarcely bring himself to make a grudging apology. After hitting the back of David Coulthard's McLaren in the rain at Spa the same year, he lost his temper in the full glare of the world's media. Yet the driving genius still transcends his vulnerable points.

Michael himself offers the most straightforward explanation of his own success. In his view, he has a mental margin, in that he does not need to use all of his brainpower in the heat of Grand Prix battle. Obviously he has the balance, co-ordination and talent which is needed to be a top driver, but he is not a man who lies awake trying to analyse why he exerts such superiority over his frustrated rivals.

'Look, the ability I have is a natural thing,' he explains. 'I don't work at it, and I don't have to make big preparations before I get into the car. I just do up the straps, start the engine, let in the clutch – and do what I do.' All the other drivers must find themselves wishing that it were all so blindingly straightforward.

Schumacher does not lie awake at night wondering why he is quick: 'I just do up the straps, start the engine and do what I do…'

Damon Hill

WHEN DAMON HILL FOUND HIMSELF partnered alongside Ayrton Senna at the start of the 1994 World Championship season, nobody in Formula 1 envied him his job. In only his second season of Grand Prix racing, this son of a famous father found himself ranged against the man many felt to be the best driver ever. But was Hill intimidated? Not for a minute.

'What do people think Ayrton is going to do to me?' he inquired, deadpan. 'Apply a Vulcan mind grip or something?' They were words that echoed the solid pragmatism of his late father, Graham, winner of the World Championship in 1962 and 1968. One of

Britain's great sporting heroes of the post-war era, Graham was killed in an air crash when Damon was only 15. But Damon inherited his father's philosophy that you should get on with the job without being seen to be complaining. In due course he would emulate his father's achievements, winning his first Grand Prix in 1993 and, three years later, becoming the only second-generation World Champion in the sport's history. His reward for scaling such peaks of achievement was to be sacked by the Williams team, after a series of events which have never been seriously explained.

Damon's mother, Bette, supports her son's career as much as she did his late father Graham's.

The relationship between Hill and Michael Schumacher deterioated during the 1994–95 seasons. Attempts at reconciliation were deemed hypocritical by the world's media.

Best seat in the house?
Hill's Williams 'office'
was consistently
competitive
during 1994–96.

Along the way, he was forced to embrace the role of team leader at Williams after Ayrton Senna's fatal accident at Imola in 1994. He rose to the occasion in magnificent style, and came within a point of the World Championship before being eliminated by Schumacher's Benetton during the final, decisive, round in Australia. Most observers believed that Schumacher, having damaged his car by glancing a wall, took the only option that would save his title hopes, and deliberately rammed Hill's Williams. Damon kept his counsel on the matter for almost four years, until 1998, when he made some remarks that conveyed the unambiguous impression that he also believed Michael was to blame. Damon had accumulated a great deal more experience behind the wheel of a Grand Prix car, and was much more aware of Schumacher's technique. Any temptation to give Michael the benefit of the doubt seemed to have completely evaporated.

Interestingly, Hill started out life with no particular ambitions to be a racing driver. From his early teens he was far more interested in motor cycling, and simply regarded father Graham's job as 'winning the Monaco Grand Prix.' I have always been left with the impression that, while Damon respected his father, he did so from a distance rather than from a position that might be described as close-knit affection. I suspect this is because Graham was killed before any serious bonding could take place with the teenager. It has also been suggested that Damon feels a sense of burning indignation that his father's death – and the insurance irregularities that arose in its aftermath – effectively bankrupted the family and left his mother facing hard times. There may be some truth in this.

The Englishman rode
a storm of criticism in
1995, bouncing back in
1996 to win the World
Championship in
emphatic style.

Either way, he carved his own distinctive niche in life. He raced motorcycles with some success at club level in the early 1980s, before his mother paid for him to attend a racing car school in France. He raced in Formula Ford and Formula 3 (winning the 1988 British Grand Prix support race at Silverstone), and ultimately graduated to Formula 3000, where he showed considerable speed but also encountered more than his fair share of mechanical failures. For 1992, he accepted an offer from Williams to succeed Mark Blundell as the official test driver. It was also understood that if regular drivers Nigel Mansell or Riccardo Patrese were sidelined for any reason then Hill would take over as their deputy; that never happened.

Instead, Hill honed his skills on empty circuits in front of empty grandstands. He relished the contribution he was making to the development of the superbly competitive Williams FW14B, but realised that he was not being given the chance to drive the machine for fun. 'I am not asked to drive the best car in Formula 1 today for my own personal pleasure,'

he confessed. 'A test session has nothing like the excitement or glamour of a Grand Prix. Even so, it can be immensely fulfilling. Each time a Williams-Renault wins, it's my win in a way as well.'

In the absence of anything else to race, he drove the uncompetitive Brabham-Judd BT60 in the early races of 1992, but the team went bust before the end of the season. It was difficult to see where he would fit into the equation for the following year, but then Mansell fell out with Frank Williams and stomped off to tackle the CART series. After careful debate, Damon was selected to drive alongside Alain Prost for the 1993 season.

It was a dream come true: to have raced in only a handful of races, in the slowest car in the field, and then to be promoted to the fastest. Hill acquitted himself admirably during that first season, finishing third in the World Championship and winning no fewer than three races. Even with Senna arriving to take over from Prost the following season, Damon's prospects looked upbeat.

Sacked by Williams, Hill's move to Arrows seemed to ignore the basic premise of motor racing that there are no miracles in this business.

The move to Jordan in 1998 seemed suspect at first, but victory in the wet at Spa-Francorchamps changed all that.

A fortnight later he won the Spanish Grand Prix. It steadied the team's nerves. He went on to win again at Silverstone, and again at Spa, Monza and Portugal. But he found himself very much in a no-win situation. Michael Schumacher, the title points leader, had been suspended from the Italian and Portuguese Grands Prix for various rule infringements, but the pressure lay – paradoxically enough – on Damon. To have a chance of the Championship, he had to win the two races from which the Benetton driver was absent. He did everything that was required of him, but Schumacher used a psychological stick to beat him with, implying that Hill was a second-class contender and that this was the reason Williams were paying big bucks for the veteran Nigel Mansell to return.

Damon's crisp response might well have come from his father's lips. 'I think it's a bit of a half-baked attempt to destabilise me,' he grinned. 'And he'll have to do better than that if he wants to succeed.' Although Schumacher won his comeback race, the European Grand Prix at Jerez, Hill bounced back into contention by beating the Benetton ace fair and square in Japan. They went into the final race a single point apart, leaving that infamous collision to decide the Championship in Schumacher's favour.

Hill was shaken by the German's tactics, but he emerged occupying the moral high ground. He was also shrewd enough not to put the boot in on his rival. He remained outwardly magnanimous and dignified, whatever he might have felt inside. It all combined to leave Michael feeling slightly uncomfortable and sheepish.

Unfortunately, Damon was unable to capitalise on this slight edge during 1995. The Williams FW17 was unreliable, and so was Hill's driving. At Silverstone and Monza he rammed into Schumacher while battling for position, and at Hockenheim he unaccountably flew off the road while leading at the end of the opening lap. By the time the team got to Suzuka, tensions were at boiling point beneath the seeming orderly surface of Williams. Lack of faith in Damon's ability was coming close to being voiced publicly. And yet again he spent most of the weekend flying off the road.

The decision was taken. At the end of 1996, Hill's services would be dispensed with and the German rising star, Heinz-Harald Frentzen, was signed up in his place. Nobody has ever been able to explain why Williams – with the best car in the pack – should have found it necessary to commit to a driver more than a year ahead of his first race. Or, indeed, to explain why the team did not come clean with Hill until he was on the verge of clinching the World Championship in 1996.

Damon started as he meant to go on in 1996, winning the first Championship Australian Grand Prix

You had to admire the strength of character that he displayed after Senna's death. Williams, that team which had seen pretty well everything before, seemed to rock on its very foundations. At Monaco, where the pressure on Hill was arguably greater than anywhere else – given his father's record of five wins in that race – the team ran just a single car. It all went wrong for Damon, who was out on the opening lap of the race. It was another terrible weekend, with Sauber's Karl Wendlinger critically injured in a huge practice accident, but I was impressed with Hill's candour. He summed up the meeting in starkly realistic terms: 'The whole thing is awful, a very sorry situation,' he said. 'The sooner we get away from Monaco and back to some semblance of normality, the better it will be.'

to be held at Melbourne's Albert Park circuit. For most of the season he drove flawlessly, despite a handful of slips in the second part of the year which allowed his team-mate, Jacques Villeneuve, to close dangerously on him going into the final race. Yet with everything to play for in that shoot-out at Suzuka, Hill drove perfectly, storming into the lead from second on the grid and never being headed. But even by the time he took the chequered flag, Damon had made a huge error of judgement in selecting his new team for 1997.

Instead of accepting an offer from Jordan, he went to the Tom Walkinshaw-run Arrows-Yamaha squad. It seemed a decision that ignored the basic premise of Grand Prix racing, namely that there are no miracles in this business. The team's historical lack of achievement was matched only by the poor track record of the Yamaha V10. Yet somehow everybody wanted to believe, for Damon's sake. Walkinshaw had judged that his team's Bridgestone rubber would provide Hill with a performance edge on several occasions. In fact it did so just once, at Budapest, where he led the Hungarian Grand Prix decisively before dropping to second place on the last lap.

It was clear to most people that this little partnership would only last a single season. Hill then took a second look at the Jordan package and concluded that the team's additional investment in research and development made it an attractive proposition. Yet initially this looked like another shaky alliance. The new Mugen-Honda engined car took some time to develop and there were some depressing moments when Hill must have feared that his competitive days were behind him. Not so. Jordan, Mugen-Honda and Goodyear all raised the standard of their game throughout 1998, to the point that Damon was able to head home his team-mate, Ralf Schumacher, for a Jordan 1–2 at the end of an incident-packed Belgian Grand Prix.

'There was a danger at one point that Jordan was always going to be left an outsider, knocking on the door and never quite getting through,' he reflected. 'But I think they went up a step on commitment and professionalism. Also, Eddie (Jordan) took key steps in that direction on the administrative front. I think, in a way, recognising what they had to do to improve the performance was a bit like an alcoholic recognising he has a problem before he can address it. This is what Jordan did in 1998.'

Hill announced his retirement from Formula 1 halfway through 1999. At 38, after 22 victories and one World Championship, the motivation had clearly gone. At least at Spa, a favourite haunt of the Racer, he had proved that he could still get the job done.

The eyes have it. Hill confirmed that nice guys could succeed at the highest levels of the sport.

Jacques Villeneuve

JACQUES VILLENEUVE'S CAREER as a Grand Prix driver began just as his father Gilles' had ended 14 years earlier, with second place in a race during which a signal from the pits played a crucial role.

Back in 1982, Gilles had seemed on course for victory in the San Marino Grand Prix at Imola, leading a Ferrari grand slam ahead of his team-mate, Didier Pironi. Yet the Frenchman played dirty, ignoring the convention within Maranello that required its drivers to hold station when they assumed a 1–2 lead, and robbing the French Canadian of victory on the final lap. Likewise in Melbourne, for his Grand Prix debut, Jacques dominated proceedings. But he damaged an oil pipe while leading the race and wisely responded to instructions from the Williams pit to ease back and settle for second rather than risk blowing his Renault V10 engine sky-high in the closing stages.

In that respect, one is tempted to suggest that Jacques displayed a level of restraint that did not always feature on his father's CV. But the old man would surely have approved. Jacques came close to winning the World Championship in his first season with Williams. Second time round he got the job done. Nobody had won a Formula 1 title earlier in his career.

When he burst onto the Grand Prix scene, in a summer test for Williams during 1995, the Formula 1 fraternity was enormously impressed. The kid had his head screwed on pretty firmly. He was formally courteous, but in no way overawed by the business of Grand Prix racing. To him, the Williams FW17 was just another racing car. One to be tamed.

It was inevitable that enormous media attention would follow every move of a man with such a famous surname. Yet, just like Damon Hill, Jacques found this irksome. Here he was, fresh across the Atlantic as reigning Indycar Champion, and all the press wanted to talk about was how he related to the achievements of a father who was killed when he was 11 years old. If he adopted a 'that was then, this

The 1997 Williams was undoubtedly the best car on the grid, and Villeneuve made the most of it.

is now' attitude, this was surely not unreasonable. He made it clear that he wanted to remain his own man. And he did not have to wait long before demonstrating that he could drive a Williams-Renault as quickly as, if not quicker than, Damon Hill. This opened another dimension to the debate over his

capability. Some people thought he did brilliantly to qualify on pole position for his first Grand Prix. Others noted that he was only beating Damon Hill, so what was all the fuss about?

It was no secret that Jacques was fast-tracked into the Williams Grand Prix team thanks in part to some

Villeneuve in consultation with his race engineer, Jock Clear. His preference for an ultra-stiff chassis set-up raised a few eyebrows at Williams.

solid assistance from Bernie Ecclestone. The FIA Vice-President fancied the idea of spicing up the field with an import from the US domestic series, and if it turned out to be the reigning Champion, then that was all the better for the media exposure such a transfer would attract.

Qualifying on pole in Melbourne inevitably led to hysterical speculation that the man could walk on water. Not so. You had to bear in mind that Jacques was the best-prepared novice in Grand Prix history, with several thousand miles of pre-season testing under his belt. It should not be forgotten that Mario Andretti was on pole position for the 1968 US Grand Prix at Watkins Glen with minimal experience of the Lotus 49 under his belt. The same could be said for Carlos Reutemann, at Buenos Aires in 1972, with the Brabham BT34.

So he went into battle, both in 1996 and 1997, with technically the best car in the business. By and large, he drove it brilliantly. His win at the Nürburgring, beating Michael Schumacher fair and square in only his fourth Grand Prix, was by any standards a terrific performance. And if the Williams team didn't quite understand his desire for an ultra-stiff chassis set-up or his off-duty 'high grunge' dress code, then they quickly recognised that here was a man blessed with unusual flair. One could almost say that he would have been a more deserving World Champion in 1996, when he carried the battle with Damon right to the last race of the season. There was also his wonderful lunge round the outside of

Schumacher's Ferrari on the final corner at Estoril in 1996. Forget the fact that Michael was wrong-footed by a Minardi. One is bound to wonder whether Damon Hill would have even thought about it.

Villeneuve's 1997 season kicked off on the wrong foot when he was bundled off the circuit at the first

Above and left A born Racer: Villeneuve's driving style has echoes of his late father, Gilles. Comparisons between the two were inevitable, but not always welcomed by Jacques.

The 1998 Williams FW20 was a disappointment, but Villeneuve continued to grab it by the scruff of the neck and make the best of a bad situation.

corner of the Australian Grand Prix. Yet he still came away from Melbourne feeling confident, as he had been fastest by far in qualifying. Then it was off to South America where he produced brilliantly judged victories in both Brazil and Argentina. Back in Europe, he won the Spanish Grand Prix, a tactically complex race that set great store on the sympathetic use of tyres.

Unaccountably, the pressure then got to him. He spun off on the second lap at Montreal, in front of his adoring home crowd, and doubters began to predict that this was the beginning of the end. Jacques had cracked. But they were wrong. He gathered everything together and bounced back with victories in the Britain, Hungary, Austria and Luxembourg. Unquestionably, he was on a roll.

Away from the cockpit he was not always as circumspect as he might have been when it came to protecting his own interests. Describing the proposed 1998 narrow track, grooved tyre regulations as 'shit' caused him to be summoned to Paris to explain himself in front of the Formula 1 governing body. Moreover, the implementation of the one race ban that so scrambled his prospects in Japan was, at the end of the day, just deserts for passing four waved yellow flags during the course of the season. In that respect, Jacques should have been more worldly wise.

Williams appealed against exclusion from the Suzuka race, and Jacques competed, but he knew full well that he would later be excluded. Schumacher won this race and with Jacques scoring no points, the Ferrari driver went into the final race – the European

Grand Prix at Jerez – one point ahead of the Canadian. Being a natural renegade, these circumstances brought the absolute best out in him. He qualified on pole position, but it was Schumacher who took the lead on the run to the first corner. In fact, Heinz-Harald Frentzen's Williams was second at the end of the opening lap and it was lap eight before Jacques got through into second place and began to steady the Ferrari driver's advantage.

With 22 of the race's 69 laps left to run, Villeneuve made a bid for the lead down Schumacher's inside going into a tight 180-degree corner. Despite pre-race warnings from the governing body that there should be no questionable tactics involved in the outcome of the Championship, Schumacher turned in towards the Williams, the Ferrari's right front wheel making smart contact with the Williams' left sidepod. Jacques stuck to his guns and got through the gap, leaving Schumacher to spin to a halt in the gravel trap. By finishing a steady third, slowing to conserve his car, Villeneuve put the Championship to bed successfully. It was a thoroughly deserved success, bearing in mind that the odds throughout the season looked uncomfortably as though they had been stacked against him for much of the time.

Resolutely his own man, Jacques had displayed a consistent determination to compete exclusively on his own terms. Yet even for one of the best drivers in the world, it is a strategy strewn with potential pitfalls. And there were still doubters. Veteran team owner Ken Tyrrell continued to rank him second to Michael Schumacher in terms of pure talent.

'Michael stands a little bit taller than the next best man,' he said. 'When I look across at the Schumacher/ Villeneuve battle, I see just Schumacher. If you put them both in the same type of car, Michael would win all the races.

'Don't misunderstand me. Jacques is very good, but I rank him with the likes of Mika Hakkinen, Damon Hill and Giancarlo Fisichella – equal at the head of the second group.'

Another who knows a great driver when he sees one is Jo Ramirez, the McLaren Formula 1 Team Co-ordinator who became a close personal friend of both Ayrton Senna and Alain Prost when they drove together for the team in 1988 and 1989. During 36 years in racing, Ramirez has also worked with the likes of Dan Gurney, Pedro and Ricardo Rodriguez, Jackie Stewart, François Cevert and Emerson Fittipaldi. He too believes Schumacher is in another class compared with Villeneuve.

'I still think Michael is streets ahead as a driver,' he said. 'He very seldom makes mistakes and certainly doesn't collapse under pressure. Jacques does. I think we all knew in 1997 that if Williams won the championship, it would be because Ferrari – not Michael – lost it.'

'Michael won two races in the dry that season because Williams messed up. He won two more in the wet, because he is the better driver. Jacques definitely had the better car, but he cannot compare as a driver.'

In my views these are harsh judgements. Schumacher may have the edge, but I doubt it is quite as decisive or clear-cut as these men may suggest. Villeneuve embarked on his third season as a Williams driver in 1998 motivated to retain his Championship crown. Unfortunately, the new FW20 was not up to scratch and the team was left to grind through a disappointing year, the first for a decade during which it failed to win at least a single Grand Prix. By the middle of the season it was clear that his enthusiasm for the situation was waning dramatically. In no way could he underestimate the long-term potential offered by Williams, but he was impatient for more success as quickly as possible. Williams would be saddled with Mecachrome engines until the end of 1999 and, if he was to use one of these power units, then he judged it would be better to move to the new British American Racing team, founded by his old friend and manager Craig Pollock.

In many ways, this audacious decision encapsulated Jacques's laid-back attitude to life. Sure, he wants success, but the fascination of thumbing his nose at the establishment and going for an untried package was too tempting to ignore. He put more store on being happy than anything else, and driving for Pollock meant that he would be operating in an environment where he felt more relaxed and understood than he ever did at Williams.

'Jacques is more pumped up than I've ever seen him in all the years I've known him,' said Craig Pollock after Villeneuve's first test in the new BAR. By the time you read these words, we will know whether or not the great gamble has paid off.

The new British American Racing team provided Villeneuve with an environment where he could truly be his own man.

Mika Hakkinen

MIKA HAKKINEN BEGAN THE 1998 FORMULA 1 World Championship season as he meant to go on. By winning. He started the process at the beginning of March, at the Australian Grand Prix, and by the time he took the chequered flag at Suzuka seven months later, he had won exactly half of the season's 16 races to become only the second Finnish driver to take the title crown. He also drove to maturity during the course of his Championship campaign. He had only posted his first Grand Prix win – at his 96th attempt – in the final race of 1997, but he used that success as the launching pad for a season-long challenge.

Hakkinen appreciated that his first win was a long time coming. By the time he won the 1997 European Grand Prix, at Jerez, he was beginning to believe that his maiden Formula 1 victory would never arrive: 'I would fly to all the races in 1998 thinking to myself 'we're gonna win this one,' he recalls. 'But there were times that I didn't think it would happen. And when I finally did win, I was surprised that I didnt feel

quite so elated as I might have expected. Then I realised this was because, inwardly, I felt that I should have been winning Grands Prix as a matter of course for a long time. So it did not perhaps have quite the impact. It was normal.'

That said, Hakkinen admits that if he hadn't scored that first victory at the end of 1997, he would have been under even greater pressure at the start of what was to prove his title season. 'It would have created more pressure,' he said, 'but, as things transpired, winning in Melbourne at the beginning of 1998 was not a surprise. It just seemed natural.'

Quiet, slightly introspective and blessed with a gentle, dry sense of humour, Mika Hakkinen made few mistakes in 1998. He also handled the pressure of racing wheel-to-wheel with Michael Schumacher for the title crown. In short, the story of 1998 was Hakkinen's deft brilliance behind the wheel of the McLaren-Mercedes MP4/13, which was itself the most formidable car of the year.

Hakkinen shone during his debut season for Lotus, 1991, and earned a reputation as a young charger.

Opposite page **Hakkinen joined McLaren in 1993 as the test driver. He was promoted to the race team when Michael Andretti left and promptly outqualified his team-mate, Ayrton Senna, on his very first outing.**

Barcelona, 1995. Mika's qualifying accident crash at Adelaide a few months later marked a turning point in his career and, indeed, his life.

Watching the celebrations on the podium at Suzuka, it was hard to believe that only three years had passed since Hakkinen came close to death, after crashing heavily in practice for the Australian Grand Prix at Melbourne. He was coaxed back to fitness thanks to the loyalty and affection of the McLaren-Mercedes team and in particular his wife Erja (then his girlfriend), whom he married a couple of months into the 1998 season.

Yet at the start of 1996 there were people in Formula 1 who believed that Mika's career was effectively written off. He may have recovered from the trauma of the injuries sustained in his accident, but he certainly didn't look the same man. Drivers who come that close to the edge don't always make a full recovery. Gone was the easy and open demeanour, and in its place came a strained and preoccupied look. His eyes, apparently extremely sensitive to light, were usually hidden behind dark glasses. Frankly, he looked like a man who was struggling to keep his spirits up. Yet his speed behind the wheel of the McLaren-Mercedes seemed unaffected, at least initially. At Melbourne in 1996 he finished a fine fifth ahead of Mika Salo's Tyrrell. But it took some time before he could admit to himself that he was really and truly 100% recovered.

'I think it is a little difficult to pinpoint precisely when I felt totally better,' he agreed. 'I don't think there was a single day when I got up in the morning and felt 'right, I'm my old self again.' It was a more gradual process. What you have to remember is that Formula 1 is a very athletic sport, and you have to sustain a high level of fitness throughout the season.

'My problem was that, after I was released from hospital in Adelaide, I spent a long time at home without doing any training. Then, when the doctors finally gave me permission to start my training program again, I suddenly realised that, all through that time of inaction, I had also been losing a degree of my mental performance.

'I was really quite down, so when the season started I was faced with the challenge of making progress with both my body and my mental state. I was certainly not 100% in Melbourne. Every day I steadily felt better, and the business of driving was causing me no problem.'

Hakkinen admits that he was slightly disappointed with the performance of the McLaren MP4/11 in the early races of the 1996. He had worked enormously hard to regain his fitness and returned to racing hoping that he would be able to challenge for race wins from the outset. As a consequence,

By the time McLaren's long-time sponsors, Marlboro, were replaced by West, Hakkinen was back to full fitness.

The 1997 season saw Hakkinen score his first Grand Prix victory, albeit with help from his team-mate David Coulthard.

The sensational MP4/13 finally gave the 'Flying Finn' an opportunity to display his true worth as a driver.

when he found the team only in a position to run in the region of fifth or sixth place, it was dispiriting. These were not the results he wanted and, by Imola and Monaco, it became clear that he was not performing at his best.

'I had to think through all the problems, because much of the trouble was with me rather than the car,' he reflected. 'The fact of the matter was that I was trying to work so hard on specific areas of the car's performance that I had somehow lost sight of the overall picture.'

After Monaco things started to change for the better and, by the time the Formula 1 circus arrived at Silverstone, the Finn believed they were making firm progress. 'Everybody in this business knows very well that it just doesn't matter whether you are third or fourth,' he pondered. 'Winning is the only thing anybody wants to hear about.'

Shrewdly managed by Keke Rosberg, Finland's first World Champion, Hakkinen had rightly judged back at the start of 1993 that it was better to be a test driver with possibly the best team in the Grand Prix business than to accept a lesser position elsewhere. When American star Michael Andretti left Formula 1 after the 1993 Italian Grand Prix, Hakkinen moved into the McLaren team full-time.

Mika had been a man to watch ever since he made his Grand Prix debut for Lotus in 1991. But he was a raw young charger in those days and, although he was tutored diligently by the Lotus Team Manager, Peter Collins, it was at McLaren that he got the opportunity to bring his talent to full flower. His McLaren debut came at Estoril, for the Portuguese Grand Prix, where he outqualified team-mate Ayrton Senna. The Brazilian driver was highly impressed, if slightly irked. In the race, Mika ran

He matured as both man and driver after winning the 1998 World Championship.

strongly before crashing. Nevertheless, everybody knew he had the touch.

There is an intensely personal dimension to the Hakkinen-McLaren relationship which made his Championship success such a special event. It was a year in which mutual trust and confidence paid off. Even more so than Ayrton Senna, Hakkinen is Ron

Dennis's protege. From day one the Finn had been taken to the team's heart. In 1998, they finally gave him the equipment to deliver in relentless and uncompromising style.

Watching Hakkinen at speed in the McLaren MP4/13 was to witness a driver totally in harmony with the car beneath him. If his maiden victory was

189

MIKA HAKKINEN

Hakkinen's wife, Erja, nursed him through the aftermath of the Adelaide crash. They were married in Monaco – where they live – in 1998.

His faultless drive around the streets of the principality in the same year was particularly impressive.

slightly fortunate, no such criticisms could be laid at his door since then. From the moment he took pole position at Melbourne and accelerated into the lead at the first corner, Hakkinen seemed to be walking on air. He beat his team-mate, David Coulthard, at Interlagos and Barcelona to set the tone of a season during which he consistently gained the upper hand. His winning run at Monaco was almost flawless, free from David's challenge after an engine failure intervened, and from then on he always seemed the stronger McLaren performer.

Not that his run to the title was error-free. He made a crucial slip at Silverstone, albeit not before he'd proved that Schumacher doesn't have a monopoly when it comes to wet weather genius, and at Magny-Cours, where he was frustrated by Eddie Irvine's presence between himself and race leader Schumacher. McLaren finger trouble cost him possible wins at the Hungaroring and at Monza, where his performance in driving the final laps to finish fifth with only rear brakes operative was rightly acclaimed as heroic. Part of his success at McLaren is his natural air of deference when he is out of the cockpit. Strapped inside the car it is a different story, and his victory over Schumacher in the Luxembourg Grand Prix was a defining moment for him.

Having been boxed into third place during the opening stages, Mika got through to second place and gained almost ten seconds on the leader, Schumacher, before vaulting ahead of him during the first spate of refuelling stops. The German's body language at the end of the race seemed to suggest that he couldn't understand how Mika had pulled such a stunt. It seemed the Grand Prix equivalent of a conjuring trick with the timing equipment. But it was none the less real for all that. Mika saw it differently. In his mind it was merely a public demonstration of what he always knew he could achieve. If anything, he handled the pressure even better than his key rival. On the starting grid at Suzuka, he walked across to the pole position Ferrari and shook Michael Schumacher's hand. It was the generous-minded gesture of a man who knew that he had nobody to fear.

The McLaren-Mercedes team felt broadly the same. At around the time of the final race of the 1998 World Championship, rumours began to circulate that Ron Dennis was keen to conclude a deal that would see Hakkinen commit to the team for the remainder of his Grand Prix career. If Ferrari could do the same for Schumacher, it certainly made sense for McLaren to take a similar approach towards its own most valuable human asset.

Mika Hakkinen is living proof of the fact that the spirit of the Racer – which harks back to the age of Ascari, Fangio, Moss et al – has survived into the 21st century.